ITALIAN FAMILY COOKING

Mary Reynolds

Hamlyn

London · New York · Sydney · Toronto

CONTENTS

ACKNOWLEDGEMENTS
The Author and Publisher would like to thank the following for their co-operation in supplying colour photographs for this book:
Birds Eye Frozen Foods Limited pages 28 and 29, 52 and 53.
Grants of St. James's pages 56 and 57.
White Fish Authority pages 60 and 61.
Remaining photographs by courtesy of PAF International
Photography by Christian Délu
Line drawings by John Scott Martin

Published by
THE HAMLYN PUBLISHING GROUP LIMITED
London   New York   Sydney   Toronto
Astronaut House   Feltham   Middlesex
© *Copyright The Hamlyn Publishing Group Limited 1974*
ISBN 0 600 38092 0
Printed in England by Cox & Wyman Ltd, London, Fakenham and Reading

USEFUL FACTS AND FIGURES

NOTE ON METRICATION

In this book, quantities have been given in both metric and Imperial measures. Exact conversion from Imperial to metric measures does not usually give very convenient working quantities and so for greater convenience we have rounded off metric measures into units of 25 grammes. The table below shows recommended equivalents:

Ounces/fluid ounces	Approx. g. and ml. to nearest whole figure	Recommended conversion to nearest unit of 25
1	28	25
2	57	50
3	85	75
4	113	100
5 ($\frac{1}{4}$ pint)	142	150
6	170	175
7	198	200
8 ($\frac{1}{2}$ lb.)	226	225
9	255	250
10 ($\frac{1}{2}$ pint)	283	275
11	311	300
12	340	350
13	368	375
14	396	400
15 ($\frac{3}{4}$ pint)	428	425
16 (1 lb.)	456	450
17	484	475
18	512	500
19	541	550
20 (1 pint)	569	575

Note When converting quantities over 20 oz., first add the appropriate figures in the centre column, *then* adjust to the nearest unit of 25. As a general guide, 1 kg. (1000 g.) equals 2.2 lb. or about 2 lb. 3 oz.; 1 litre (1000 ml.) equals 1.76 pints or almost exactly 1$\frac{3}{4}$ pints.

Liquid measures

The millilitre is a very small unit of measurement and we felt that to use decilitres (units of 100 ml.) would be easier. In most cases it is perfectly satisfactory to round off the exact conversion to the nearest decilitre, except for $\frac{1}{4}$ pint; thus $\frac{1}{4}$ pint (142 ml.) is 1$\frac{1}{2}$ dl., $\frac{1}{2}$ pint (283 ml.) is 3 dl., $\frac{3}{4}$ pint (428 ml.) is 4 dl., and 1 pint (569 ml.) is 6 dl. For quantities over 1 pint we have used litres and fractions of a litre.

Tablespoons

You will note that often measurements are given in tablespoons; the spoon used is the British Standard measuring spoon of 17·7 millilitres. All spoon measures are level.

Oven temperatures

The chart below gives the Celsius (Centigrade) equivalents recommended by the Electricity Council.

Description	Fahrenheit	Celsius	Gas Mark
Very cool	225	110	$\frac{1}{4}$
	250	130	$\frac{1}{2}$
Cool	275	140	1
	300	150	2
Moderate	325	170	3
	350	180	4
Moderately hot	375	190	5
	400	200	6
Hot	425	220	7
	450	230	8
Very hot	475	240	9

NOTES FOR AMERICAN USERS

In the recipes in this book quantities are given in American standard cup and spoon measures as well as Imperial and metric measures. The list below gives some American equivalents or substitutes for terms used in the book.

British	American
dough or mixture	batter
frying pan	skillet
greaseproof paper	wax paper
grill	broil
kitchen paper	paper towels
liquidiser	blender
loaf tin	loaf pan
minced	ground
muslin	cheesecloth
stoned	pitted
whisk	beat/whip

Note The British pint is 20 fluid ounces as opposed to the American pint which is 16 fluid ounces.

The recipes in this book are arranged in regions, therefore to find soups, sauces, desserts, etc., see index.

LET'S EAT LIKE THE ITALIANS

This is a collection of simple but colourful recipes of the kind an Italian mama cooks for her family. Traditionally, Italian housewives, often with large families and limited means, have excelled at making the best possible use of locally produced foods. In many regions this often meant little or no meat. From them we can borrow many ideas for making a little meat go a long way, for cooking vegetables imaginatively, and for achieving originality in everyday dishes with unexpected additions of herbs, cheese, spices, lemon, capers, nuts and anchovies.

Mealtimes are happy social occasions when the family gathers to talk and enjoy mama's cooking. Main meals usually consist of at least three courses starting with either an antipasto to whet the appetite or, more substantially, with a soup or a dish of rice or pasta. In Italy, rice and pasta dishes are generally served as a separate course rather than as an accompaniment. The main course might be meat, fish, poultry, offal or just cheese, with a vegetable dish or salad. Invariably meals end with fresh fruit followed by a small cup of strong black coffee.

Italians love explaining in detail exactly how you should make their traditional dishes (each version differing slightly from the last of course!), emphasising the correct texture of the rice or pasta, the quality of the olive oil or vegetables, and how you can turn the left-overs into tomorrow's speciality! No wonder Italians all over the world retain such a nostalgic affection for mama's cooking!

Because traditional Italian cooking is based on local produce it varies enormously from region to region, and dramatically from North to South. In the northern cattle-rearing regions butter is the favourite cooking fat, but where the olive tree flourishes – in Liguria and the South – olive oil takes over. Tuscany, with an ample share of both is the great divide. Pasta is unquestionably the national dish but preferences for different types of pasta are regional. The north is the home of the flat noodle type, usually made from a dough containing eggs, and still often made at home. The same type of pasta is rolled into sheets, stuffed and cut into shapes for ravioli, tortellini, and a whole tribe of stuffed pastas. And how excellent they are when made with delicate pasta and rich but light fillings. South of Rome the manufactured pastas like spaghetti and macaroni take over, olive oil rather than butter becomes the favourite dressing, and sauces become more robust and colourful.

Rice and maize are both northern crops and polenta (ground maize) and rice dishes the staple 'filling' foods right across the north of Italy. Their popularity diminishes as you travel southwards, and in Tuscany it isn't difficult to guess that the local crop must be the small white beans which appear in so many dishes.

To encourage tourists to ask for local specialities, the recipes in this book have been grouped under regions. For unless visitors expect to find and try regional foods, they will be given what Italians *think* we want . . . more spaghetti, tomato sauce, stewed veal and cheese. In time food everywhere will become 'tourist European' and half the fun of travelling will be lost for ever. So, each chapter starts with brief notes on the best wines, food and cheeses of the region followed by some dishes you can reproduce at home. Sadly, less than justice has been done to the excellent fish dishes found all around the coast simply because it is virtually impossible to find the kinds and variety of fish to make them here.

Italian food and recipe names are confusing and the same item can be known by different names in different regions. To sort out this confusion a comprehensive guide to buying food and eating in all parts of Italy is the answer, such as 'Eating Italian' by Spike and Charmian Hughes.

Enjoy your cooking, and don't be too concerned about sticking slavishly to the recipe. Italian mammas add a little more of this or a little less of that according to what is in season or good value at the time – or just because that's how they like it!

CHOOSING ITALIAN WINES

Italy produces more wine than any other country in the world. The majority is consumed in Italy but exports are increasing all the time, and nowadays your local wine merchant will stock many of the wines mentioned in this book.

Until recently, Italian wines have been confusing to buy because the districts of origin were not defined, quality was variable, and the same names seemed to apply willy nilly to white or red, dry or sweet wines. But in 1963 a law controlling the name and origin of wines was passed, and this classification is now appearing on an ever increasing number of wine labels. There are three standards:

Denominazione Semplice This rating is a simple statement of the region of production e.g. Piedmont, Tuscany, etc. There are no set standards and it applies only to lesser wines.

Denominazione di Origine Controllata The D.O.C. rating is reserved for wines of 'particular reputation and worth'. If a wine carries the D.O.C. on its label you can be sure it comes from the area named, that the vintage date is correct and the approved methods of production have been used. Such a wine will have reached agreed standards of quality.

Denominazione Controllata e Garantita The D.O.C.G. rating is for really outstanding wines. No wine has yet been awarded this grade, but several have their applications under consideration.

Grapes grow everywhere in Italy and when travelling around the country it is more interesting and usually cheaper to try the local wines first. The best known of these are listed in each of the regional chapters, but unnamed carafe wines are the cheapest of all and may turn out to be excellent value.

There's only one way to find out!

Useful label language

Riserva better quality and vintage wines · *Classico* from the best area of its region · *Imbottigliato all'origine* estate bottled · *Fiasco* flask · *Vini da banco, Vino ordinario, Vino da tavola* ordinary carafe wine, not usually bottled *Bianco* white · *Rosso* red · *Nero* dark red · *Chiaretto* light · *Rosato* pink · *Secco* dry · *Amaro* bitter or very dry · *Amabile* sweet · *Abboccato* medium sweet · *Dolce* very sweet · *Spumante* sparkling · *Frizzante* semi-sparkling · *Vino Santo* sweet wine made from sun dried grapes · *Cotto* cooked · *Stravecchio* very old and mellow · *Vino liquoroso* very sweet wine

Cooking with wine

In Italy, wine is a local ingredient which has been sloshed into cooking pots since Roman times, much to the advantage of tough pieces of meat and stringy chicken. Frequently a dry white wine is used, but for game, red meat and certain fish stews a robust red wine is preferred. When wine is added to stewed or braised dishes the meat is first lightly browned in fat, then the wine is poured over and reduced to almost nothing by rapid boiling, before the stock is added and the slow cooking commenced. By this means the wine permeates the meat and helps to tenderise as well as flavour it.

Marsala This is used frequently not only in sweet dishes but also for chicken, veal and even ham or vegetable dishes. A bottle of inexpensive Marsala is a good culinary investment as the wine keeps perfectly even after the bottle has been open for months.

Vermouth Dry white vermouth is excellent in recipes calling for both white wine and herbs. Use about half as much as you would of a table wine.

FLAVOURS OF ITALIAN COOKING

More than any others the following ingredients will help you to capture the flavour, colour and texture of the dishes you have enjoyed in Italy. Most of them are fairly easy to find – if not in delicatessen stores and greengrocers then in specialist Italian shops – and their availability is increasing all the time as trade within the common market expands.

Cheese

Many dishes owe their special character to the unique cooking qualities of certain Italian cheeses. This doesn't mean you cannot use other cheeses but the dish will not be quite the same. The three cheeses extensively used in Italian cooking are Parmesan, Mozzarella and Ricotta.

Parmesan A hard piquant cheese whose rich flavour enhances every dish it is added to. Expensive, but worth every penny as a little goes a long way. The most economical way of buying it is by the piece, say half to one pound at a time. If kept loosely wrapped in polythene in the refrigerator it will keep for months and can then be freshly grated just before use, thus retaining all its flavour. When buying Parmesan look for a golden colour and a rough grainy texture. Cheese branded 'Parmigiano Reggiano' are considered the best. Another hard spicy cheese often used instead of Parmesan in Italy, and sometimes available here, is *Pecorino Sardo*. In the absence of either use a mature, dry Cheddar.

Mozzarella A rather rubbery, tasteless curd cheese sold wrapped in small packages dripping with whey. It melts readily and is much used in Southern Italy specially for pizza. *Bel Paese* melts readily, too, and is a useful substitute.

Ricotta A soft white curd cheese used in stuffings and sauces, for gnocchi and as a sweet pastry filling. It must be eaten fresh. Substitutes are English curd cheese, or home-made cream cheese which can be made as follows:
Home-made cream cheese
Scald all the equipment to be used. Heat 2 pints (generous 1 litre, 5 cups) milk to a little above blood heat (38°C. or 100°F.), pour into a bowl, add the juice of a lemon and leave until a curd forms – 15–20 minutes. Line a colander with damp muslin and spoon the curd into it. Tie up and hang over a bowl to drain for 2–3 hours. Scrape from the muslin, add salt if required and store, covered, in the refrigerator for not longer than 2–3 days. Makes about 8 oz. (225 g.) cream cheese.

Garlic

Although not used lavishly in Italian cooking it is an important flavour in many recipes. A few bulbs wrapped in foil will keep for months in the refrigerator without anyone knowing they are there. The cloves vary in size so quantities are a matter of taste.

Herbs

Many dishes owe their distinctive flavour to the generous use of herbs. Use fresh herbs when possible but dried are useful too. The kinds used most frequently in Italian cooking are parsley, sage, mint, rosemary, marjoram (and its wild cousin oregano), bay leaves and basil. All but the last grow readily in English gardens and even basil can be made to flourish in a warm and sheltered spot or a sunny windowsill. Buy dried herbs in small amounts and replace frequently. Oregano is available in a useful 'shaker' jar.

Lemons

Lemons are indispensable in the Italian kitchen. The juice or rind goes into innumerable dishes, and chops and steaks, as well as fish, are served with wedges of lemon.

Meat products

Italian cured meats are available fresh, in polythene pre-packs and sometimes canned.
Prosciutto Crudo A delicately cured ham, eaten raw and thinly sliced often with ripe melon or fresh figs. Delicious but expensive. The best comes from Parma or St. Daniele
Pancetta Rolled cured belly pork. Cheaper but coarser than prosciutto. Eat raw or use for cooking.

Coppa Small roll of cured pork shoulder. Sliced raw and eaten like salame.

Mortadella Huge cooked sausage of smoothly ground meats, laced with pork fat and flavoured with spices.

Salame Long sausages of mixed lean meats and pork fat, all coarsely chopped and spiced according to variety. There are various qualities but *Salame Milano* is considered the best.

Cotechino A rich, lightly cured pork sausage weighing 1–2 lb. (½–1 kg.). Among Italians, a partially cooked cotechino needing only 15 minutes simmering in water is popular. Serve in thick slices, hot with lentils or beans, cold with salad.

Zampone The cotechino mixture stuffed into an empty pigs foot, and weighing from 3–4 lb. (1½–1¾ kg.). Cook and serve as for Cotechino. Also available partially cooked.

Salamelle Slightly dried, pinkish sausage filled with coarsely chopped pork. Boil or fry.

Luganeghe Fresh pork sausages in a continuous casing, usually displayed in a coil. Fry, grill or stew.

Pasta

Italians are very particular about the cooking and serving of pasta. There are hundreds of kinds, shapes and names of pasta so nothing less than a book can do justice to the subject. But assuming you are cooking manufactured, rather than home-made pasta, these are the general points to ensure success.

1 Check the label to be sure you are buying good quality pasta made from pure hard Durum wheat.
2 Choose a *large* pan, allowing about 6 pints (3½ litres, 15 cups) salted water (1 tablespoon to 3 pints (1½ litres, 7½ cups)) per 1 lb. (½ kg.) pasta.
3 Don't add the pasta until the water is boiling really fast, then add gradually stirring a few times. Long spaghetti or macaroni needs to be eased into the pan and coiled around as it softens.
4 Keep the water boiling fast and strain immediately the pasta is cooked 'al dente' – that is to say when the pasta is tender but firm when you bite it. Pasta should *never* be soft or slimy. The time will vary from 4 to 14 minutes according to the size and kind of pasta; the label should give you a guide. Home-made pastas take much less time to cook.
5 Drain thoroughly in a colander. Then return to the pan with a little butter or olive oil (about 1 oz. (25 g.)

or 2 tablespoons to 12 oz. (350 g.) pasta, or more if you like) plus 1 to 2 tablespoons of grated Parmesan, and toss lightly together. Turn into a *heated* dish and serve *immediately*, with more grated cheese handed separately.

To reheat pasta Pasta is difficult to keep hot. The best way of coping with successive servings is to slightly undercook the pasta, drain it and let it get cold. To reheat simply drop the required amount into fast boiling water. In less than a minute it will be hot, separate and ready to drain and serve.

Quantities Appetites vary, but 3 oz. (75 g.) per person is average.

Rice

Good quality Italian rice absorbs a lot of liquid and produces the correct creamy texture for a risotto. *Arborio* and *Vialone* are two reliable kinds to ask for. They take about 20 minutes to cook.

Miscellaneous items

Anchovy fillets in oil These are used a great deal in Italian cooking. Small (1¾ oz./45 g.) cans are a useful standby.

Capers A popular ingredient in the sauces and salads of the South. Bottled capers keep well even after opening.

Dried mushrooms These give a most distinctive flavour to sauces and are ready to use after 15 minutes soaking. Buy freshly imported Italian *porcini* which should be pale fawn in colour. If brown they are stale. Cook for about 20 minutes only.

Olives Black or green olives are cheaper when bought loose and will keep for a week in the refrigerator. Revitalise shrivelled black olives by covering with olive oil for a few days. The remaining oil will be deliciously fruity and excellent for salad dressings and pizzas.

Olive oil This is essential to the flavour of many dishes, and in Italy a light olive oil is used for frying. When buying, larger quantities work out cheaper, and if kept tightly stoppered in a cool place it will last for months. Other cooking oils can be used but the flavour of the dish will be a little changed.

Pine nuts These give an original texture to various small pastries and some meat or vegetable dishes. Available at health food stores.

Tunny fish in oil A useful store cupboard ingredient which occurs in many recipes. Various size cans are available.

Salt and pepper Use coarse sea salt, and black peppercorns freshly ground in a peppermill.

Tomatoes Peeled plum tomatoes in cans are invaluable for sauces and cooking generally, and are usually much cheaper than fresh tomatoes. Tubes of concentrated tomato purée are useful for adding in *small* amounts to strengthen and colour various dishes.

Vinegar Only wine vinegar is used in Italian cooking.

Vegetables

Quantities of colourful vegetables are one of the great joys of shopping and cooking in Italy. The variety is enormous and the ways of serving them diverse and ingenious. A vegetable dish can be served as an antipasto or, combined with small amounts of meat, as a main course. Crisp, dressed salads are popular with or after the principal dish. The following are especially typical of the Italian kitchen:

Courgettes (Zucchini) These succulent baby marrows from 3 to 6 inches (7½–15 cm.) long are cooked unpeeled, just wiped and topped and tailed. Tiny ones can be cooked whole, middle size ones sliced crosswise or lengthwise and sautéed or fried in various ways, and used in risottos, soups and omelets. Larger ones are excellent stuffed and baked.

Aubergine (Melanzane) In the South these dark shiny truncheons are favourites for frying or stuffing. To fry, cut, unpeeled, into ¼ inch (½ cm.) thick slices or cubes, sprinkle with salt and leave in a colander to drain for an hour. Rinse and pat quite dry before frying.

Fennel (Finocchio) The pale green bulb of Florentine fennel is used in Italy rather than the feathery foliage. Its crisp texture and delicate aniseed flavour is much appreciated when eaten raw at the end of a meal, or as a salad ingredient. It is delicious cooked too, braised in stock or with cheese (see page 47).

Globe artichokes (Carciofi) This decorative vegetable needs to be young and tender for most Italian methods of cooking them. Tiny whole artichokes are preserved in oil, middle sizes are stewed in oil and wine, fried, or sliced and dressed for salad; and large ones are stuffed. Canned artichoke hearts make attractive meal starters or omelet fillings.

Sweet peppers (Peperoni) Given time the familiar green pepper ripens through yellow to rich red. The flavour is very mild provided you get rid of the white seeds and pithy core. They can be stewed, stuffed or grilled, and *raw* finely sliced pepper gives a lovely crisp bite to mixed green or rice salads. To peel peppers grill them briskly, turning frequently, until the skin begins to blister and blacken, then peel and rinse in cold water.

SOME BASIC RECIPES

These are a few of the sauces and basic recipes used throughout Italy, and referred to in other chapters.

SALSA DI POMIDORI
Tomato sauce using canned tomatoes

A rich and rough textured sauce which needs no skinning of tomatoes or sieving at the end. It freezes well.

Serves 3–4

IMPERIAL/METRIC	AMERICAN
3 tablespoons oil	scant $\frac{1}{4}$ cup oil
1 clove garlic, peeled	1 clove garlic, peeled
1 (14 oz./400 g.) can peeled tomatoes	1 (14 oz.) can peeled tomatoes
2 tablespoons tomato purée	3 tablespoons tomato paste
sugar	sugar
salt and pepper	salt and pepper

Heat the oil and garlic *gently* in a pan for several minutes until the oil is well flavoured. Discard the garlic. Add the tomatoes and their juice, tomato purée, sugar and seasonings to taste. Cover and simmer gently for at least 40 minutes, stirring occasionally. Adjust the consistency as necessary, adding water if too thick, or boiling rapidly to reduce if too thin. Beat briskly to break up any large pieces of tomato, check the seasoning and use as required.

BESCIAMELLA
Béchamel sauce

Makes $\frac{1}{2}$ pint (3 dl., $1\frac{1}{4}$ cups) sauce

IMPERIAL/METRIC	AMERICAN
1 oz./25 g. butter	2 tablespoons butter
1 oz./25 g. flour	$\frac{1}{4}$ cup all-purpose flour
$\frac{1}{2}$ pint/3 dl. hot milk	$1\frac{1}{4}$ cups hot milk
salt and pepper	salt and pepper
grated nutmeg	grated nutmeg

In a small saucepan melt the butter over low heat. Add the flour and, using a wooden spoon, stir and cook very gently for 2 minutes. Off the heat add the milk little by little, beating well to a smooth sauce. Stir until boiling, then simmer for 10 minutes. Season well with salt, pepper and nutmeg.

SALSA DI CARNE
Meat sauce

A basic meat sauce for pasta or gnocchi, or to mix with vegetables and cheese for a pie. A little dry wine or Vermouth, chopped mushrooms or parsley are good additions. A useful standby sauce to keep in the freezer.

Serves 4–5 with pasta

IMPERIAL/METRIC	AMERICAN
2 oz./50 g. onion, peeled	2 oz. onion, peeled
2 oz./50 g. carrot, peeled	2 oz. carrot, peeled
1 stick celery	1 stalk celery
2 tablespoons oil	3 tablespoons oil
8 oz./225 g. minced raw beef	1 cup ground raw beef
½ oz./15 g. flour	2 tablespoons all-purpose flour
½ pint/3 dl. stock	1¼ cups stock
2 teaspoons tomato purée	2 teaspoons tomato paste
salt and black pepper	salt and black pepper

Prepare the vegetables and chop *finely*. Heat the oil in a saucepan and fry the vegetables gently for 5 minutes, stirring frequently. Add the meat and stir and fry briskly until it changes colour. Stir in the flour and cook another minute or so. Add the stock, tomato purée and seasonings to taste. Simmer gently for 30–40 minutes, uncovered, but stirring from time to time. Check seasoning and use as required.

MAIONESE
Mayonnaise

Italians make excellent mayonnaise using their best olive oil, and lemon juice rather than vinegar.

Serves 4

IMPERIAL/METRIC	AMERICAN
2 egg yolks	2 egg yolks
1 teaspoon salt	1 teaspoon salt
2–3 teaspoons lemon juice	2–3 teaspoons lemon juice
scant ¼ pint/1½ dl. olive oil	⅔ cup olive oil

All the ingredients must be at room temperature. Put the yolks into a small basin (standing on a cloth to prevent slipping). Add the salt and 1 teaspoon of lemon juice mixing in thoroughly with a small wooden spoon or wire whisk. Stirring vigorously all the time, add the oil drop by drop until the sauce begins to thicken. Then increase the flow to several drops at a time and finally a thin thread, stirring continuously until all the oil is used. If the sauce becomes too thick thin it with lemon juice or water. The final consistency should be thick and shiny.

MAIONESE TONNATA
Tunny fish mayonnaise

This is an excellent sauce for coating hard-boiled eggs, cold sliced chicken or veal or for filling hollowed out tomatoes or cucumbers. You can make it using a quick blender or traditional method.

IMPERIAL/METRIC	AMERICAN
1 (3½ oz./100 g.) can tunny fish	1 (3½ oz.) can tuna fish
3 anchovy fillets	3 anchovy fillets
2 egg yolks	2 egg yolks
2–3 teaspoons lemon juice	2–3 teaspoons lemon juice
¼ pint/1½ dl. olive oil	⅔ cup olive oil

Blend the tunny fish, anchovy fillets, egg yolks and lemon juice in an electric blender, then add the oil slowly in a thin stream to form a thick creamy sauce.

Without a blender, press the tunny fish and anchovy fillets through a sieve, and then stir by degrees into a mayonnaise made previously by the recipe above.

PASTELLA
A crisp frying batter

IMPERIAL/METRIC	AMERICAN
4 oz./100 g. plain flour	1 cup all-purpose flour
large pinch salt	large pinch salt
$\frac{1}{4}$ pint/1$\frac{1}{2}$ dl. tepid water	$\frac{2}{3}$ cup tepid water
2 tablespoons olive oil	3 tablespoons olive oil
1 large egg white	1 egg white

Sift the flour and salt into a basin. Stir in the water and oil, forming a smooth, fairly stiff batter. Beat well and leave in a cold place for 1–2 hours. Immediately before using, whisk the egg white to a light foam and fold gently into the batter.

RISOTTO BIANCO
White risotto

This is a basic family risotto to which other ingredients such as cooked chopped ham, chicken, sausage, shellfish or vegetables can be added towards the end of the cooking.

Serves 3–4

IMPERIAL/METRIC	AMERICAN
2 oz./50 g. butter	$\frac{1}{4}$ cup butter
4 oz./100 g. onion, chopped	1 cup chopped onion
10 oz./275 g. Italian rice	scant 1$\frac{1}{2}$ cups Italian rice
1$\frac{3}{4}$ pints/1 litre hot stock	4$\frac{1}{4}$ cups hot stock
grated Parmesan	grated Parmesan
salt and pepper	salt and pepper

Heat half the butter in a saucepan and fry the onion *gently* until soft. Add the rice and stir until translucent. Add the hot stock in 3 or 4 instalments, adding more as the previous addition becomes absorbed. Cook over medium heat, uncovered, stirring from time to time. Towards the end of the cooking time (20–25 minutes using Italian rice) stir continuously to avoid sticking. When the rice is creamy but still a little firm in the centre, and the liquid almost absorbed, the risotto is ready. Stir in the remaining butter, 1 heaped tablespoon of Parmesan and salt and pepper to taste. Serve with more butter and Parmesan handed separately.

POLPETTE
Fried meat balls

Italians make these light meat balls from raw minced beef or veal, or from cooked leftovers. Polpette freeze and reheat well.

Serves 4

IMPERIAL/METRIC	AMERICAN
2 oz./50 g. white bread	2 oz. white bread
little milk	little milk
2 small eggs	2 eggs
12 oz./350 g. raw minced meat	1$\frac{1}{2}$ cups firmly packed raw ground beef
1–2 cloves garlic, peeled	1–2 cloves garlic, peeled
$\frac{1}{2}$ teaspoon grated lemon rind	$\frac{1}{2}$ teaspoon grated lemon rind
1 oz./25 g. grated Parmesan	$\frac{1}{4}$ cup grated Parmesan
little chopped parsley	little chopped parsley
salt and pepper	salt and pepper
nutmeg	nutmeg
oil for frying	oil for frying

Soak the bread in milk for 10 minutes. Beat the eggs in a basin, add the meat, crushed garlic, lemon rind, cheese, parsley, with salt, pepper and nutmeg to taste. Squeeze the bread dry, add to the other ingredients and mix all together lightly but thoroughly. With well floured hands, form the mixture into small egg shapes and flatten slightly but do not compress – the polpettes should remain light. Heat $\frac{1}{4}$-inch ($\frac{1}{2}$-cm.) depth of oil in a frying pan and fry the polpette, turning once, until cooked through and crisp outside. Drain on absorbent paper and serve hot with salad.

TURIN AND PIEDMONT

The traditional cooking of Piedmont is a curious combination of the robust fare of mountain folk and the sophisticated cuisine of an aristocracy of French origin. Agriculture flourishes in the plains and in addition to various cereals Piedmont is the great rice producing area of Italy. In fact, rice and polenta (a kind of thick porridge made from maize flour) is to Northern Italians what pasta is to the Southerners. Locally grown vegetables include asparagus, celery, peppers, artichokes and onions, and in spite of the Northerly latitude, grapes, peaches and strawberries flourish. Chocolate confectionery, candied chestnuts and biscuits are specialities of the towns. In the cold mountain regions, the food becomes very substantial and boiled meats and highly seasoned garlicky dishes are popular. Chamois, game and even wild boar or wild goat can be found in season.

THE WINES

To the south of Piedmont sunny vine clad hills produce some of the finest red wines of Italy, as well as a great quantity and variety of local wines, both red and white. It is also the home of Vermouth.

Red wines

Barolo
Big, full bodied wine, somewhat rough when young but becoming mellow and velvety with age.

Barbaresco
Similar to Barolo but lighter and quicker to mature.

Gattinara
Similar to Barolo but lighter and more elegant when aged.

Nebbiolo
Sound red wine improved with age. There are sweet and sparkling varieties of this wine.

Barbera
Dark gutsy wine which goes well with highly seasoned food. Also found as a sweetish and slightly '*frizzante*' dessert wine.

Freisa
Commonly found wine, garnet red and usually dry. But there is a sweet sparkling variety.

Grignolino
Lightish red wine to drink young, cool and slightly '*frizzante*'. Also good when aged.

Dolcetto
Found in many districts, usually dryish, but sometimes semi-sweet or sparkling.

Barbera d' Asti
Sparkling semi-sweet deep red wine. Refreshing if slightly chilled.

White wines

Asti Spumante
The famous semi-sweet aromatic sparkling white wine. Serve chilled for parties, or with the sweet course.

Moscato d' Asti
Sweeter and usually cheaper version of the above, much loved by Italians.

Cortese
Light, dry and refreshing white wine.

Vermouth

Vermouth is a blend of wines fortified with spirit, and flavoured with worm-wood and various '*estratti*' – extracts of herbs, tree barks, roots, fruit rinds or berries. Brands differ considerably but the main types are either '*bianco*' – sweet white, '*rosso*' – sweet red, or 'dry' – white wine.

SOME FOOD SPECIALITIES

Agnelotti
Small stuffed pasta served with a meat sauce, melted butter and grated cheese.

Bollito
Various meats boiled together in one huge pot.

Camoscio
Chamois meat cooked in a very tasty sauce.
Costolette alla valdostana
Veal cutlet with cheese, egg and crumbed and fried.
Finanziera di pollo
Chicken giblets, sweetbreads, mushrooms and truffles cooked in a thick meat sauce.
Gnocchi alla Fontina
Semolina dumplings boiled in spiced milk containing melted cheese, then rolled in breadcrumbs and fried.
Grissini
Slender bread sticks made in Turin.
Mocetta
Salted and preserved chamois (Valle d'Aosta).
Rane dorate
Fried frogs legs.
Riso e ceci
Broth of rice and chick peas with tomatoes and spice.

Tartufi bianchi
Large fragrant 'white' truffles, usually grated raw in wafer thin slices. In reality these pale brown truffles are found around Alba from October to January. Also found in Tuscany and Romagna.

CHEESE

Fontina
Rich cows' milk cheese made in flat wheel shapes. A table cheese which melts creamily and is the basis of the famed *Fonduta* – cheese fondue.
Robiole
Creamy goats' milk cheese, slightly spicy.
Tomini
Goats' milk cheese with pepper.
Pagliarini
Rather sharp cows' milk cheese sold on straw mats.

MINESTRA PIEMONTESE
Piedmont style soup

A thick, nourishing vegetable soup, typical of country cooking and excellent for cold weather fireside suppers.

Serves 4

IMPERIAL/METRIC	AMERICAN
1 stick celery	1 stalk celery
2 small leeks	2 small leeks
1 small carrot	1 small carrot
2 pints/generous 1 litre chicken stock	5 cups chicken stock
3 oz./75 g. rice	scant ½ cup rice
2 egg yolks	2 egg yolks
2 tablespoons chopped parsley	3 tablespoons chopped parsley
2 tablespoons cold water	3 tablespoons cold water
grated Parmesan cheese	grated Parmesan cheese
salt and pepper	salt and pepper

Prepare the vegetables. Chop the celery, slice the leeks and grate the carrot, then simmer together in the stock for 20 minutes. Stir in the rice, cover and cook until the rice is tender. In a large tureen, beat together the egg yolks, parsley, water and 1 oz. (25 g.) grated cheese. Gradually pour on the boiling soup, stirring briskly all the time. Check the seasoning and serve at once, with more grated cheese handed separately.

LA BAGNA CAUDA
A 'Hot bath' dip

A robust, garlicky hot sauce into which you dunk pieces of crisp raw vegetables. In Piedmont, cardoons (edible thistles) are often one of the vegetables.

Serves 4

IMPERIAL/METRIC	AMERICAN
various raw vegetables*	various raw vegetables*
6 cloves garlic	6 cloves garlic
6 anchovy fillets	6 anchovy fillets
4 tablespoons olive oil	⅓ cup olive oil
2 oz./50 g. butter	¼ cup butter
bread sticks	bread sticks

* celery, carrot, sweet pepper, fennel, etc.

Cut the vegetables into sticks of about ½ × 2 inches (1 × 5 cm.) long and leave them to crisp in the refrigerator. Chop the garlic and the anchovy fillets finely. When ready to serve, heat the oil and butter in a flameproof casserole, add the garlic and anchovy and simmer gently for 10 minutes. Transfer the casserole to a spirit lamp in the centre of the table and arrange the vegetable and bread sticks around. To eat, simply dip a piece of vegetable in the *bagna cauda*. Wash down with rough red wine.

SALSA VERDE
Green sauce

A refreshing, sharp green sauce to serve with hot boiled meat or with cold meats.

IMPERIAL/METRIC	AMERICAN
1 level tablespoon capers	1 level tablespoon capers
1 clove garlic	1 clove garlic
1 shallot	1 shallot
2 oz./50 g. fresh parsley	2 oz. fresh parsley
3 tablespoons olive oil	scant $\frac{1}{4}$ cup olive oil
1$\frac{1}{2}$ tablespoons lemon juice	2 tablespoons lemon juice
salt and black pepper	salt and black pepper

Drain the capers, peel the garlic and shallot and wash and dry the parsley. Chop all these together finely or pass through a mouli grater or electric blender. Put into a basin, stir in the oil, lemon juice and seasonings and mix thoroughly together as for a French dressing. Chopped anchovy fillets can be added to the sauce.

PEPERONI ALLA PIEMONTESE
Stuffed peppers

A tasty and colourful meal starter for garlic lovers. Don't overcook the peppers, they should retain a little crispness.
Serves 4

IMPERIAL/METRIC	AMERICAN
4 sweet peppers	4 sweet peppers
4 large tomatoes	4 large tomatoes
2 cloves garlic	2 cloves garlic
4 anchovy fillets	4 anchovy fillets
4 tablespoons olive oil	$\frac{1}{3}$ cup olive oil

Select 2 green and 2 yellow round shaped peppers. Cut lengthwise in half and discard the pith and seeds. Wash and drain, and place hollow sides up in a shallow ovenproof dish. Skin and quarter the tomatoes, put 2 pieces in each pepper. Peel and crush the garlic and mix thoroughly with the mashed anchovy fillets and the oil. Pour a little of this mixture into each pepper. Cook, uncovered (350°F., 180°C., Gas Mark 4) for 30–35 minutes. Serve cold.

TROTELLE ALLA SAVOIA
Baked trout Savoy style

Trout abound in the lakes and streams of Piedmont. This is a popular way of serving them.
Serves 4

IMPERIAL/METRIC	AMERICAN
8 oz./225 g. button mushrooms	2 cups button mushrooms
4 trout, 8–12 oz./225–350 g. each	4 trout, $\frac{1}{2}$–$\frac{3}{4}$ lb. each
salt and pepper	salt and pepper
little flour	little flour
3 oz./75 g. butter	6 tablespoons butter
1 tablespoon oil	1 tablespoon oil
1 teaspoon lemon juice	1 teaspoon lemon juice
1 oz./25 g. dry white breadcrumbs	$\frac{1}{2}$ cup dry white bread crumbs
2 spring onions	2 scallions

Wipe the mushrooms and slice finely. Preheat oven to 400°F., 200°C., Gas Mark 6. Wash the trout, leaving the heads and tails on, and pat dry. Season with salt and pepper and coat evening with flour. Heat 1 oz. (25 g.) butter and oil in a large frying pan and fry the trout for 3 to 4 minutes each side, browning lightly. In a smaller pan, melt another 1 oz. (25 g.) butter and fry the mushrooms with the lemon juice and $\frac{1}{4}$ teaspoon salt until beginning to soften. Spread the mushrooms in an ovenproof dish and lay the trout side by side on top. Fry the breadcrumbs in the pan in which the fish was cooked, adding more butter if necessary, and when crisp, spoon over the trout. Bake in the preheated oven for 10 minutes. Meanwhile, fry the sliced spring onions for a minute in the remaining butter and scatter over the trout before serving.

INVOLTINI DI CAVOLO
Stuffed cabbage leaves

For this dish use whole outside leaves from a large green cabbage, cutting away any tough stalk or mid-rib. The minced meat can be beef, lamb or pork.

Serves 3–4

IMPERIAL/METRIC	AMERICAN
9–12 cabbage leaves	9–12 cabbage leaves
1 slice white bread	1 slice white bread
2 tablespoons oil	3 tablespoons oil
3 oz./75 g. onion, chopped	¾ cup chopped onion
1 stick celery, chopped	1 stalk celery, chopped
12 oz./350 g. minced raw meat	1½ cups firmly packed ground raw meat
1 large egg, beaten	1 egg, beaten
1 oz./25 g. grated Parmesan	¼ cup grated Parmesan
salt and black pepper	salt and black pepper
½ pint/3 dl. meat stock	1¼ cups meat stock

To garnish

chopped parsley	chopped parsley
tomato quarters	tomato quarters

Soften the cabbage leaves by plunging them into boiling, salted water for 5 minutes. Drain, rinse in cold water and gently spread flat. Soak the bread in cold water. Heat the oil in a saucepan and gently fry the onion and celery until soft. Off the heat, mix in the meat, egg, cheese, bread which has been squeezed dry, and salt and pepper to taste. Put a spoonful of stuffing in the centre of each leaf and roll up like a parcel turning the sides inwards. Squeeze gently in the hands to firm the shape and arrange side by side in a shallow flameproof dish. Pour the stock over the 'parcels', cover and simmer very gently for about 1 hour. Serve in the same dish sprinkled with parsley and garnished with pieces of tomato.

Illustrated in colour on page 20

MANZO STUFATO AL BAROLO
Beef braised in Barolo

Serves 6

IMPERIAL/METRIC	AMERICAN
2 lb./1 kg. braising beef	2 lb. stewing beef
½ bay leaf	½ bay leaf
salt	salt
ground black pepper	ground black pepper
grated nutmeg	grated nutmeg
½ bottle Barolo*	½ bottle Barolo*
2 oz./50 g. bacon fat	2 oz. fat back
4 oz./100 g. onion, chopped	1 cup chopped onion
2 cloves garlic, peeled	2 cloves garlic, peeled
* Or any robust red wine.	

Cut the meat into pieces about ¼ inch (½ cm.) thick and 2 inches (5 cm.) square. Put into a basin with the bay leaf, a little salt, pepper and nutmeg, and the wine. Cover and leave to marinate for at least 5–6 hours. Then remove the meat and drain well. In a flameproof casserole, heat the bacon fat and fry the onion and garlic gently until golden. Add the pieces of meat and cook for a few minutes, stirring frequently, until the meat changes colour. Strain the marinade over the meat, cover the casserole with kitchen foil and the lid; simmer over a *very* low heat for about 2 hours, until the meat is tender and the sauce thick and rich. Remove any surplus fat from the surface and serve the meat and sauce on a hot dish.

INSALATA DI RISO
Rice salad

Locally grown asparagus is combined with rice and other vegetables to make this attractive salad.

Serves 4

IMPERIAL/METRIC	AMERICAN
6 oz./175 g. Italian rice	scant 1 cup Italian rice
4 oz./100 g. green asparagus (cooked or canned)	¼ lb. green asparagus (cooked or canned)
2 sticks celery	2 stalks celery
2 oz./50 g. button mushrooms	½ cup button mushrooms
1 white truffle (optional)	1 white truffle (optional)
few drops Marsala	few drops Marsala
6 tablespoons mayonnaise (page 10)	½ cup mayonnaise (page 10)
little thin cream	little coffee cream

Cook the rice in plenty of boiling, salted water until *just* tender, then drain and dry thoroughly and leave to become cold. Meanwhile, clean and prepare the vegetables, cutting the asparagus into short lengths, finely slicing the celery, mushrooms and truffle if used. Just before serving, stir the Marsala into the mayonnaise and enough cream to make a pouring consistency. Add all the other ingredients, reserving half the asparagus, and mix together lightly. Arrange in a shallow bowl, and garnish with pieces of asparagus.

PESCHE RIPIENE
Stuffed baked peaches

Serves 4

IMPERIAL/METRIC	AMERICAN
4 macaroons	4 macaroons
4 large peaches	4 large peaches
1 egg yolk	1 egg yolk
2 oz./50 g. castor sugar	¼ cup sugar
1 oz./25 g. soft butter	2 tablespoons soft butter
1–2 teaspoons lemon juice	1–2 teaspoons lemon juice

Crush the macaroons and put into a basin. Cut the peaches in half, discard the stones and scoop out enough pulp to create a deep space for stuffing. Add the pulp to the macaroon crumbs together with the egg yolk, sugar, butter and enough lemon juice to moisten. Mix thoroughly and divide between the peaches, smoothing it into a mound. Arrange the peaches in a well buttered, ovenproof dish and bake in a moderate oven (350°F., 180°C., Gas Mark 4) for 30–35 minutes. Serve hot or cold.

CILIEGE AL BAROLO
Cherries in red wine

Serves 3–4

IMPERIAL/METRIC	AMERICAN
1 lb./½ kg. red cherries	1 lb. red cherries
4 oz./100 g. sugar	½ cup sugar
strip orange rind	strip orange rind
pinch cinnamon	pinch cinnamon
1 tablespoon redcurrant jelly	1 tablespoon red currant jelly
¼ pint/1½ dl. Barolo*	⅔ cup Barolo*

* Or any full bodied red wine.

The cherries should be ripe, large and preferably Morellos. Wash, remove stalks and stone them if you wish. Meanwhile, put the rest of the ingredients into a saucepan, heat gently until the sugar dissolves then boil for 1 minute. Add the cherries and simmer for 10–15 minutes. Remove the drained cherries to a serving dish, reduce the syrup by boiling rapidly for several minutes then strain over the cherries. Serve hot, warm or chilled, as you please.

Braised marrow bones (Ossobuco) (page 23)

MILAN AND LOMBARDY

Lombardy stretches south from the Alps to the river Po and includes the breathtaking scenery of the Italian lakes. Acres of tranquil pasture graze dairy herds whose milk supports a vast cheese industry. Lombardy cheeses such as Gorgonzola, Bel Paese and Dolcelatte are world famous. Agriculture flourishes too, and the grain crops, vegetables and veal are of high quality. The traditional cooking of Lombardy although substantial is more refined and less garlicky than in the South. In Milan, however, restaurants are virtually international as in so many industrial cities. Butter is the favourite cooking fat and rice and polenta, rather than pasta, the principal 'filling' foods. Veal is cooked in a variety of interesting ways and you certainly will not be hungry after a Milanese version of *Fritto misto*. Snails, frogs and game are popular; the lakes supply perch, pike and carp as well as other freshwater fish. Chestnuts and almonds are considerable crops and are used in puddings and confectionery. Don't leave Lombardy without sampling a real risotto. Unlike a pilau, a typical risotto is essentially creamy in texture, the result of using good quality Italian rice which absorbs a lot of liquid and needs 20 to 25 minutes to cook. Italians never waste food and one of their ways of using leftovers is the 'Somersault risotto' (page 30) – which I first met not in the home of a thrifty housewife but as a 'speciality' dish in one of Milan's poshest restaurants!

THE WINES

The first three red wines listed below, all from the Valtellina Valley, are already much appreciated outside Italy. The light refreshing wines from the Western shore of Lake Garda are also enjoyed by the many visiting holidaymakers.

Red wines

Inferno
One of the best red wines of the area, especially when 3–4 years old.

Sassella
A well balanced red wine which improves with bottle age. When mature it goes well with roast red meats and game.

Grumello
Similar to Sassella.

Freccia Rosso
Sound red wine from the Valtellina.

Rosso della Riviera del Garda
Refreshing light red wine.

Chiaretto del Garda
Popular pale red wine.

White wines

Lugana
One of the best of the Lake Garda wines, pale golden and dry. Drink with local dishes and especially fish.

Tocai del Garda
Sweetish white wine.

SOME FOOD SPECIALITIES

Agoni al burro e salvia
Small freshwater fish cooked in sage flavoured butter.

Busella
Highly seasoned tripe dish.

Colomba
Easter bun containing candied peel.

Costeletta alla milanese
Veal cutlet, egg and crumbed and fried.

Mostarda
Candied fruits in a mustard syrup.

Polenta e osei
Small birds roasted and served with polenta.

Pannetone
Large, dry yeast cake containing fruit and peel.

Tinca carpionata
Fried freshwater fish marinated in wine, vinegar, herbs and garlic.
Torrone di cremona
Kind of nougat.

CHEESES

Bel Paese
Soft, bland cows' milk table cheese. It melts readily and is often used in cooking instead of Mozzarella.
Gorgonzola
Rich blue veined cheese with a softish texture. A white

version is much appreciated by Italians.
Mascarpone
Very soft cream cheese served with fruit and used to make puddings.
Robiola
Soft, rich creamy cheese from the Alpine districts. Varies from area to area.
Stracchino
A generic name covering a family of soft, smooth cows' milk table cheeses. Needs to be eaten fresh.
Taleggio
One of the stracchino tribe.

ZUPPA PAVESE
Poached egg in broth

A quickly prepared nourishing snack, said to have originated in the town of Pavia.

Serves 1

IMPERIAL/METRIC	AMERICAN
1 slice firm bread	1 slice firm bread
butter for frying	butter for frying
½ pint/3 dl. chicken broth	1¼ cups chicken broth
1 fresh egg	1 fresh egg
1 tablespoon grated Parmesan	1 tablespoon grated Parmesan

Remove the crusts and cut the bread into 4 small triangles. Fry in melted butter until crisp on both sides. Meanwhile, heat the broth to simmering point in a small saucepan. Break the egg into a saucer, slide it into the broth and poach lightly. Lift the egg into a hot soup plate and strain the broth over it. Dip the fried bread in Parmesan and arrange around the egg. Serve at once.

MINESTRONE ALLA MILANESE
Milan style minestrone

Minestrone varies from district to district and according to the vegetables in season. The Milan version contains rice rather than pasta.

Serves 6

IMPERIAL/METRIC	AMERICAN
2 oz./50 g. unsmoked fat bacon	2 oz. unsmoked fat bacon slices
1 onion, peeled	1 onion, peeled
3 sticks celery	3 stalks celery
1 large carrot	1 large carrot
8 oz./¼ kg. potatoes, peeled	½ lb. potatoes, peeled
2 courgettes	2 zucchini
3 tomatoes, peeled	3 tomatoes, peeled
8 oz./¼ kg. cabbage	½ lb. cabbage
1½ oz./40 g. butter	3 tablespoons butter
3 pints/1½ litres stock or water	7½ cups stock or water
5 oz./150 g. shelled peas	1 cup shelled peas
4 oz./100 g. rice	⅔ cup rice
2 sage leaves	2 sage leaves
1 tablespoon chopped parsley	1 tablespoon chopped parsley
grated Parmesan	grated Parmesan
salt and pepper	salt and pepper

Chop the bacon. Wash and prepare the vegetables. Chop the onion, celery and carrot. Dice the potatoes, courgettes and tomatoes, shred the cabbage. Melt the butter in a large saucepan, put in the bacon, onion, celery and carrot and cook gently, stirring frequently, for about 10 minutes. Add the potato, courgette and stock, cover and simmer for 20 minutes. Now add the tomatoes, peas, rice and finely chopped sage. Continue cooking gently for another 20 minutes. Finally stir in the chopped parsley, 2 tablespoons of cheese and seasoning to taste. Hand more cheese separately.

Stuffed cabbage leaves (page 15)

Tomatoes stuffed with scampi (page 34)

POLENTA
Maise flour porridge

This staple family food of Northern Italy is served in many ways. There should always be enough left over to fry for the next meal.

Serves 4–5

IMPERIAL/METRIC	AMERICAN
1½ pints/scant 1 litre water	3¾ cups water
2 teaspoons salt	2 teaspoons salt
8 oz./225 g. finely ground polenta	about 1½ cups finely ground polenta

Bring the water and salt to a rolling boil in a large pan. Slowly pour in the polenta, stirring all the time, until a smooth mixture forms. Reduce the heat and simmer, stirring frequently, for 20–25 minutes until the polenta resembles thick golden porridge. Serve at once with gravy, butter and grated cheese, or a tomato sauce or perhaps a small roast bird. Flat 'cakes' of cold polenta are fried and served in similar ways or sandwiched with ham and cheese.

POLENTA PASTICCIATA
Polenta pie

In addition to the polenta above, make 1 pint (6 dl., 2½ cups) béchamel sauce (page 9), flavouring it well with grated Parmesan, and fry 8 oz. (225 g., 2 cups) thinly sliced mushrooms in a little butter. In a shallow, buttered baking dish arrange alternate layers of polenta, sauce and mushrooms finishing with sauce and grated Parmesan. Bake in a hot oven until the surface is golden and bubbling. Serve at once to 6 hungry people!

PEPERONATA
Sweet peppers with onions and tomatoes

This colourful dish is equally good hot or cold and worth making in double quantities. Serve cold as an antipasto or hot with chicken, pork or veal. It reheats well.

Serves 4–6

IMPERIAL/METRIC	AMERICAN
6 large sweet peppers*	6 large sweet peppers*
1 lb./½ kg. ripe tomatoes	1 lb. ripe tomatoes
2 cloves garlic	2 cloves garlic
8 oz./¼ kg. onions, sliced	½ lb. onions, sliced
4 tablespoons olive oil	⅓ cup olive oil
salt	salt
* Red, green or mixed.	

Cut the peppers in half, discard the seeds, rinse in cold water and cut into ½ inch (1 cm.) wide strips. Skin and quarter the tomatoes, peel and slice the garlic. Heat the oil in a wide pan and fry the onion and garlic *gently* until golden. Add the peppers, stir, cover and cook gently for 10 minutes. Add the tomatoes and salt to taste. Cook uncovered, stirring frequently, until most of the liquid has evaporated and the *peperonata* is reduced to a thickish mixture – from 30 to 40 minutes cooking in all.

PEPERONATA VERDE
Green peperonata

When tomatoes are scarce and expensive, practical Italian housewives simply leave them out of the recipe! Cook a 'green' peperonata very gently, keeping the pan *covered* throughout the cooking time and stirring from time to time.

VITELLO TONNATO
Veal with tunny fish mayonnaise

An unusual, decorative and delicious dish for a cold lunch or buffet. The purpose of boning and tying the meat is to make it easier to carve neat slices.

Serves 6–8

IMPERIAL/METRIC	AMERICAN
2 lb./1 kg. boned leg of veal	2 lb. boned leg of veal
1 carrot, quartered	1 carrot, quartered
1 onion, quartered	1 onion, quartered
1 stick celery, chopped	1 stalk celery, chopped
4 peppercorns	4 peppercorns
2 bay leaves	2 bay leaves
1 teaspoon salt	1 teaspoon salt

For the sauce

IMPERIAL/METRIC	AMERICAN
Tunny fish mayonnaise (page 10)	Tunny fish mayonnaise (page 10)

To garnish

IMPERIAL/METRIC	AMERICAN
capers	capers
lemon slices	lemon slices
few black olives	few ripe olives

Have the meat tied in a neat roll. Put it into a pan with the bone, the vegetables, peppercorns, bay leaves, salt and water just to cover. Bring slowly to the boil, cover and simmer until tender – from 1½–2 hours. Remove the pan to a cool place and leave the veal to cool in the stock. Meanwhile make the tunny fish mayonnaise, thinning it if necessary with a little cold veal stock. When cold, slice the meat thinly, spread each slice with a little sauce and then arrange the slices overlapping each other on a flat serving dish. Spoon the remaining sauce over to cover the meat completely. Cover loosely with a tent of foil and refrigerate for up to 12 hours. Remove 1 hour before serving and serve sprinkled with capers, and garnished with lemon slices and olives.

OSSOBUCO
Braised marrow bones

Serves 3–4

IMPERIAL/METRIC	AMERICAN
2 lb./1 kg. meaty shin of veal*	2 lb. meaty shin of veal*
little flour	little flour
3 tablespoons olive oil	scant ¼ cup olive oil
1 small onion	1 small onion
1 small carrot	1 small carrot
1 stick celery	1 stalk celery
¼ pint/1½ dl. white wine	⅔ cup white wine
1 (15 oz./425 g.) can tomatoes	1 (15 oz.) can tomatoes
salt and black pepper	salt and black pepper

Gremolata

IMPERIAL/METRIC	AMERICAN
1 clove garlic, crushed	1 clove garlic, crushed
1 tablespoon chopped parsley	1 tablespoon chopped parsley
½ teaspoon grated lemon rind	½ teaspoon grated lemon rind

* Have the veal sawed across the bone into 2-inch (5-cm.) portions, consisting of bone and marrow with meat all around.

Coat the pieces of meat with flour and fry quickly in the hot oil until browned on each side; remove carefully, keeping the marrow in place. Prepare and slice the vegetables and fry lightly for 5 minutes in the same fat. Add the wine and bubble briskly until almost evaporated. Stir in the tomatoes and seasoning and, when simmering, replace the meat. Cover tightly and cook gently until tender – about 1½ hours. Remove the meat and keep hot in a dish. Pass the vegetables and gravy through a foodmill or electric blender and, if necessary, boil until reduced to a medium thick sauce. Check the seasoning and pour over the meat. Prepare the gremolata by mixing together the garlic, chopped parsley and lemon rind; sprinkle over the meat just before serving. Traditionally ossobuco is served with a dish of risotto Milanese but no other vegetables.

Illustrated in colour on page 17

Home-made pizza (page 39)

VERZADA CON SALSICCE
Pork sausages with cabbage

A country dish, very good made with well spiced and meaty sausages.

Serves 4

IMPERIAL/METRIC	AMERICAN
2 lb./1 kg. firm white cabbage	2 lb. firm white head cabbage
2 oz./50 g. unsmoked streaky bacon rashers	3 unsmoked bacon slices
2 oz./50 g. butter	¼ cup butter
4 oz./100 g. onion, chopped	1 cup chopped onion
2 tablespoons wine vinegar	3 tablespoons wine vinegar
salt and pepper	salt and pepper
1 lb./½ kg. Italian sausages	1 lb. Italian sausages

Cut the cabbage into quarters and wash in cold, salted water. Drain and shred finely. Derind and dice the bacon. Melt the butter in a heavy pan and gently fry the bacon and onion until the onion softens. Add the cabbage, stirring and turning to coat with fat. Cover and cook for 10 minutes. Stir in the vinegar and seasoning. Prick the sausages and bury in the cabbage. Cover tightly and cook over a very low heat for about an hour. Serve the cabbage with the sausages arranged on top.

PETTO DI VITELLO RIPIENO ALLA CASALINGA
Home style stuffed breast of veal

Serves 6

IMPERIAL/METRIC	AMERICAN
2 lb./1 kg. breast of veal	2 lb. veal breast
1 thick slice ham	1 thick slice cured ham
8 oz./225 g. pork sausagemeat	½ lb. pork sausagemeat
1 oz./25 g. grated Parmesan	¼ cup grated Parmesan
bunch chopped parsley	bunch chopped parsley
1 egg, beaten	1 egg, beaten
1 oz./25 g. butter	2 tablespoons butter
6 tablespoons white wine	½ cup white wine

Remove bones if necessary. Using the point of a sharp knife, cut a horizontal pocket for the stuffing through the centre of the meat, taking care not to break the skin. For the stuffing, cut the ham into dice and mix with sausagemeat, cheese, parsley and egg. Spoon into the veal pocket and loosely sew up the open side with a needle and white thread. Put into a buttered ovenproof casserole, spread the butter on top and pour the wine around. Cook in a moderate oven (325°F., 170°C., Gas Mark 3) for about 2 hours, basting with pan juices occasionally.

To serve, remove the thread and arrange the meat in a large dish with separately cooked cabbage and carrots around. Carve in thick slices and spoon a little of the pan juices over each portion.

PETTI DI POLLO AL MARSALA
Chicken breasts with Marsala

There is an excellent way of cooking sliced turkey breast on page 47. Either recipe can be used for chicken or turkey breasts, or for escalopes of veal.

Serves 4

IMPERIAL/METRIC	AMERICAN
4 chicken breasts	4 chicken breasts
salt and pepper	salt and pepper
flour	flour
1½ oz./40 g. butter	3 tablespoons butter
1 tablespoon oil	1 tablespoon oil
4 oz./100 g. button mushrooms	1 cup button mushrooms
grated Parmesan	grated Parmesan
6 tablespoons Marsala	½ cup Marsala
2 tablespoons chicken broth	3 tablespoons chicken broth

Free the chicken breasts of skin and bone, place between greaseproof paper on a board and flatten with a rolling pin. Dust with salt, pepper and flour. Heat 1 oz. (25 g., 2 tablespoons) butter and the oil in a heavy frying pan and fry the chicken briskly until golden on each side, then gently until cooked through. Transfer to a shallow ovenproof dish and keep warm. Wipe the mushrooms, slice finely and fry in the same frying pan. Spread on top of the chicken breasts and sprinkle generously with grated Parmesan. Pour the Marsala into the frying pan, boil rapidly until reduced by half, then stir in the chicken broth and remaining butter. Pour over the chicken and put under a hot grill for a minute or two just until the cheese melts. Serve immediately, with asparagus spears, French beans or courgettes.

RISOTTO ALLA MILANESE
Risotto Milanese style

The creamy texture of risotto is easily achieved with Italian arborio or vialone rice. Beef marrow and saffron are traditional but not essential. White wine or Marsala, about 4 tablespoons, can be added just before the stock.

Serves 4

IMPERIAL/METRIC	AMERICAN
2 oz./50 g. butter	¼ cup butter
4 oz./100 g. onion, chopped	1 cup chopped onion
1 oz./25 g. beef marrow	1 oz. beef marrow
12 oz./350 g. Italian rice	1⅔ cups Italian rice
2 pints/generous 1 litre chicken stock	5 cups chicken stock
¼ level teaspoon saffron	¼ level teaspoon saffron
grated Parmesan	grated Parmesan
salt and pepper	salt and pepper

Melt half the butter in a *thick* saucepan and fry the onion gently until golden. Add the marrow and the rice and stir until the rice is translucent. Heat the stock and add to the rice in a few instalments, adding more as soon as the last addition is nearly absorbed. Stir frequently and cook, uncovered, over moderate heat. Towards the end add the saffron dissolved in a little hot stock, the remaining butter and 1 heaped tablespoon of Parmesan. Season to taste. Serve as soon as the rice is tender but still firm, and the general consistency creamy. Cooking time with Italian rice is about 20 to 25 minutes. Serve with more Parmesan handed separately.

Pea and ham mould (page 65)

Country style risotto (page 34)

RISOTTO AL SALTO
'Somersault' risotto

A traditional Lombardy way of using left-over risotto.

Serves 1

IMPERIAL/METRIC	AMERICAN
left-over risotto	left-over risotto
little butter	little butter
grated Parmesan	grated Parmesan

Refrigerate the left-over risotto until needed, to ensure that it is cold and firm. Melt ½ oz. (15 g., 1 tablespoon) butter in a small omelette pan and put in about 2 tablespoons of risotto. Flatten to form a firm 'pancake' about ¼ inch (½ cm.) thick. Cook gently until the underside is crisp and golden. Carefully invert on to a plate, melt another ½ oz. (15 g., 1 tablespoon) butter in the pan then slip the risotto cake back to brown the other side. Serve flat with more butter and grated Parmesan.

PERE RIPIENE
Pears filled with cheese

The Italian combination of ripe pears with Gorgonzola or Pecorino cheese is a pleasant one.

Serves 4

IMPERIAL/METRIC	AMERICAN
4 ripe pears	4 ripe pears
1 tablespoon lemon juice	1 tablespoon lemon juice
1 oz./25 g. soft butter	2 tablespoons soft butter
2 oz./50 g. Gorgonzola cheese	2 oz. Gorgonzola cheese
1½ oz./40 g. nuts, chopped	scant ¼ cup chopped nuts

Peel the pears, cut lengthwise in half leaving the stalk on one side and scoop out the cores. Brush the pears inside and out with lemon juice to prevent browning. Beat the butter and cheese together until creamy and divide between the centres of half the pears. Press the 2 halves of the pear together again and roll in the finely chopped nuts. Chill before serving.

COPPE DI MASCARPONE
Cream cheese cups

Mascarpone is a cream cheese made in Lombardy, but bought or homemade cheese can be used instead.

Serves 4

IMPERIAL/METRIC	AMERICAN
8 oz./225 g. Mascarpone	1 cup Mascarpone
2 eggs, separated	2 eggs, separated
2 oz./50 g. castor sugar	¼ cup sugar
2 tablespoons liqueur*	3 tablespoons liqueur*
8 oz./¼ kg. raspberries	½ lb. raspberries
Savoy finger biscuits	ladyfingers

* An orange liqueur, or brandy.

Sieve the cream cheese into a bowl, add the egg yolks and sugar and beat until fluffy. Beat in the liqueur. Whisk the egg whites until firm then fold lightly into the cream. Pile into pretty individual dishes and stud the surface with raspberries. Small strawberries would do equally well. Serve with Savoy finger biscuits.

VENICE AND VENETO

The north-east corner of Italy includes regions to north and west of Veneto where the culinary influence is strongly Austro-Hungarian. But the food of Veneto, and particularly that of Venice, Padua, Verona and Treviso, is essentially Italian. For lovers of fish and shellfish Venice is a must. Start with an early morning visit to the fish market beside the Rialto bridge for a visual feast of unfamiliar species, bizarre shapes and splendid colours. Begin your meal with an 'antipasto fruitti di mare' consisting of various small shellfish artistically arranged with perhaps a tiny pink octopus presiding in the centre. Or, more substantially, with a fish stew or a shellfish risotto. Treviso, just to the north of Venice, is the market centre of a rich agricultural area and has a fascinating market as well as a culinary tradition of its own. It boasts, among other vegetables, a unique rose coloured winter salad known as 'radicchio rosso'. Appetites in Veneto are hearty to say the least and both rice and polenta are consumed in vast quantities. So, strangely enough, is salt cod made into various dishes. Venice lays claim to a number of regional risottos featuring fish, poultry, veal or vegetables. And also to some sturdy soups such as *Risi e bisi* (page 33) and *Pasta e fagioli* (page 33). Eels from Comacchio are greatly esteemed and several eel dishes feature among local specialities. But seafoods apart, it is the vibrant colours of the food which lingers in the memory – in Veneto you eat with your eyes.

THE WINES

Grapes, they say, were first planted in this area by the Etruscans before 400 B.C. Today it is a prolific vine region producing wines of quality and charm although lighter than those of Piedmont and Lombardy. Several of them, Soave and Valpolicella in particular, have become well known outside Italy.

White wines

Prosecco
A variable wine which comes in dry, sweet and sparkling forms.

Soave
Popular fresh and well balanced wine, best drunk young and chilled. Good with Venetian fish dishes.

Recioto Bianco
A sweet wine.

Tocai
Dry, yellowish white wine with a bitter aftertaste.

Terlano
Dry wine from the Trentino valley.

Red wines

Bardolino
Light, refreshing ruby wine, best drunk young and cool.

Valpantena
Light wine similar to Valpolicella.

Valpolicella
Popular light wine, best drunk young and cool.

Recioto amarone
Full bodied wine for roasts.

Recioto Rosso
A sweetish red wine, sometimes sparkling.

Santa Maddalena
Soft red wine from the Bolzano area.

Teroldego
Big full bodied wine from the Trentino valley.

SOME FOOD SPECIALITIES

Baccalà montecato
Purée of salt cod.

Baicoli
Dry biscuits, orange flavoured.

Mussels au gratin (page 70)

Bigoli
Spaghetti.

Bottarga
Hard roe of tunny fish eaten with oil and lemon.

Grançeole
Spider crab.

Polenta e 'osei'
Small roast birds served on polenta.

Radicchio rosso
Crisp red salad vegetable.

Sfogie in saòr
Sole with herbs and garlic.

Tacchino con sugo di melagrana
Turkey with pomegranate sauce.

Zuppa di trippa
Soup containing tripe and various vegetables.

CHEESES

Asiago
A granular, rather sharp flavoured table cheese which is used for grating when hard.

RISI E BISI
Rice with peas

Although served in a soup plate, a fork is usually supplied for eating this famous dish. Venetians insist it can be made only with very sweet, young and tender peas. Out of season, frozen petits pois are the ones to use.

Serves 4

IMPERIAL/METRIC	AMERICAN
6 oz./175 g. onion, peeled	6 oz. onion, peeled
2½ oz./65 g. butter	5 tablespoons butter
4 oz./100 g. ham or bacon	¼ lb. ham or bacon
12 oz./350 g. shelled peas	2¼ cups shelled peas
8 oz./225 g. Italian rice	generous 1 cup Italian rice
1½ pints/scant 1 litre hot stock	3¾ cups hot stock
salt and pepper	salt and pepper
grated Parmesan	grated Parmesan

Finely chop the onion and fry gently in 2 oz. (50 g., ¼ cup) butter in a wide saucepan. After 5 minutes, add the diced ham or bacon, the peas and the rice. Cook gently, stirring often, until the butter is absorbed and the rice translucent. Add the stock and seasoning to taste. Cover and simmer gently until the rice is soft and most of the stock absorbed – about 20–25 minutes. Stir in the remaining butter and a heaped tablespoon of Parmesan. Hand more Parmesan when serving.

PASTA E FAGIOLI
Bean and pasta soup

In winter for the main course a piece of unsmoked bacon or some pigs' trotters are cooked in this family soup. In summer the soup is made thinner and tomatoes are added.

Serves 4

IMPERIAL/METRIC	AMERICAN
8 oz./225 g. haricot beans	generous 1 cup navy beans
1 ham bone	1 ham bone, from cured ham joint
3 tablespoons olive oil	scant ¼ cup olive oil
6 oz./175 g. onion, chopped	6 oz. onion, chopped
1 stick celery, chopped	1 stalk celery, chopped
1 clove garlic, crushed	1 clove garlic, crushed
salt and black pepper	salt and black pepper
2 oz./50 g. ribbon pasta	2 oz. ribbon pasta
chopped fresh parsley	chopped fresh parsley
grated Parmesan	grated Parmesan

Soak the beans overnight in water to cover. Next day drain, put into a pan with the ham bone and 2 pints (generous 1 litre, 5 cups) water. Cover, and simmer until tender – 1½ to 2 hours. Discard the bone. Purée half the beans in a blender or food-mill, then return to the pan. Heat the oil in a small pan and gently fry the onion, celery and garlic until soft; add to the beans with seasoning to taste and extra water if necessary. When boiling, add the pasta broken into 1-inch (2½-cm.) pieces and cook for another 15 minutes. Stir in the parsley before serving and hand the Parmesan separately.

POMODORI RIPIENI CON SCAMPI
Tomatoes stuffed with scampi

Serves 4

IMPERIAL/METRIC	AMERICAN
1 (8 oz./225 g.) pack frozen scampi*	1 (½ lb.) package frozen jumbo shrimp*
4 large firm tomatoes	4 large firm tomatoes
salt	salt
1 recipe mayonnaise (page 10)	1 recipe mayonnaise (page 10)
2 hard-boiled eggs	2 hard-cooked eggs
4 black olives	4 ripe olives
1 tablespoon capers	1 tablespoon capers
crisp lettuce leaves	crisp lettuce leaves

* Small peeled raw scampi, *not* the breaded kind.

Illustrated in colour on page 21

Thaw the scampi then drop into simmering, salted water and cook for 2–3 minutes only, just until opaque. Drain and cool. Cut a slice off the top of each tomato, scoop out the pulp, sprinkle the case with salt and leave upside down to drain. Make the mayonnaise keeping it thick and firm. Chop the hard-boiled eggs and mix with half the scampi and the mayonnaise. Pile into the tomato cases. Add extra mayonnaise if wished then top each stuffed tomato with an olive and garnish with the remaining scampi and some drained capers. Serve garnished with crisp lettuce leaves.

Variation
POMODORI RIPIENI CON TONNO
Tomatoes stuffed with tunny fish

Chop 2 hard-boiled eggs and mix with 6 oz. (175 g.) flaked tunny fish, 2 teaspoons drained capers, 1 tablespoon chopped parsley, 2–3 tablespoons mayonnaise, a teaspoon of lemon juice and pepper to taste. Spoon into the tomato cases and top with a few black olives.

RISOTTO ALLA PAESANA
Country style risotto

Any tender vegetables in season can be used in this risotto – celery, broccoli, French or broad beans etc. The asparagus is not essential.

Serves 4

IMPERIAL/METRIC	AMERICAN
2 tablespoons olive oil	3 tablespoons olive oil
3 oz./75 g. onion, chopped	¾ cup chopped onion
2 oz./50 g. asparagus spears, trimmed	2 oz. asparagus spears, trimmed
4 oz./100 g. small courgettes	¼ lb. small zucchini
4 oz./100 g. shelled peas (optional)	¾ cup shelled peas (optional)
8 oz./¼ kg. tomatoes, skinned	½ lb. tomatoes, skinned
8 oz./225 g. Italian rice	generous 1 cup Italian rice
1½ pints/scant 1 litre chicken stock	3¾ cups chicken stock
2 oz./50 g. butter	¼ cup butter
2 oz./50 g. grated Parmesan	½ cup grated Parmesan
salt and pepper	salt and pepper

Heat the oil in a large saucepan and fry the onion *gently* for 5 minutes. Add the halved asparagus spears to the pan with the sliced courgette and the peas. Stir and cook for several minutes then add the chopped tomatoes and the rice. Stir and cook for several minutes then add hot stock in 3 or 4 instalments, adding more as the last addition is absorbed. Cook uncovered, over medium heat, stirring now and then. Towards the end of the cooking time (20–25 minutes using Italian rice) watch carefully to prevent sticking. As soon as the rice is cooked and most of the liquid absorbed, *stir* in the butter and cheese and season to taste. Serve with more cheese handed separately.

Illustrated in colour on page 29

TRIGLIE ALLA VENEZIANA
Red mullet Venetian style

Serves 4

IMPERIAL/METRIC	AMERICAN
6 oz./175 g. onion, peeled	6 oz. onion, peeled
2 tablespoons olive oil	3 tablespoons olive oil
$\frac{1}{3}$ pint/2$\frac{1}{4}$ dl. white wine	scant 1 cup white wine
1 tablespoon wine vinegar	1 tablespoon wine vinegar
4 small red mullet	4 small red mullet
fresh mint leaves	fresh mint leaves
2 cloves garlic, peeled	2 cloves garlic, peeled
orange or lemon slices	orange or lemon slices
Illustrated in colour on page 61	

Chop the onion *finely* and fry gently in the oil until soft but uncoloured. Add the wine and vinegar and boil for about 10 minutes or until reduced by half. Wash and dry the mullet and put 3 mint leaves and half a clove of garlic inside each. Make 2 crosswise incisions on each side of the fish, brush with oil and grill under medium heat for about 6–7 minutes each side. Arrange side by side on a serving dish and pour the hot sauce over them. Serve *cold*, gaily garnished with orange or lemon slices.

SCAMPI IN UMIDO
Simmered scampi

Serves 3

IMPERIAL/METRIC	AMERICAN
2 oz./50 g. butter	$\frac{1}{4}$ cup butter
12 oz./350 g. raw scampi*	$\frac{3}{4}$ lb. jumbo shrimp*
1–2 cloves garlic	1–2 cloves garlic
chopped fresh parsley	chopped fresh parsley
2 teaspoons lemon juice	2 teaspoons lemon juice

Melt the butter in a frying pan and fry prepared scampi *gently*, stirring frequently, until just cooked – from 6–10 minutes depending on size. When nearly cooked, stir in the finely chopped garlic, the parsley and lemon juice with seasoning as required. Serve with pan juices poured over.
* If using frozen scampi allow just to thaw then drain.

RISOTTO ALLA MARINARA
Shellfish risotto

Make a white risotto as described on page 11, using fish stock if possible (below). Prepare a mixture of freshly cooked shellfish such as prawns, crayfish, mussels, clams, cockles and pieces of lobster or crab – all heated gently in butter with a little finely chopped garlic and a lot of chopped parsley. Add to the risotto with the pan juices, with the final addition of butter and cheese. Stir and heat gently for a minute or so for the flavours to blend. Serve with grated Parmesan.
Fish stock is made by covering the shells and heads of scampi, prawns, lobster or crayfish with water and white wine plus onion, celery and herbs, and simmering for 30 minutes. Strain and use for fish risottos, sauces, etc.

FEGATO ALLA VENEZIANA
Liver Venetian style

Serves 4

IMPERIAL/METRIC	AMERICAN
1 lb./$\frac{1}{2}$ kg. onions, peeled	1 lb. onions, peeled
olive oil	olive oil
12 oz./350 g. liver	$\frac{3}{4}$ lb. liver
salt and black pepper	salt and black pepper
1 lemon, quartered	1 lemon, quartered

Slice the onions finely and fry gently in a large frying pan in enough oil to well moisten the base of the pan. They will take about 15 minutes to become soft and golden. Meanwhile with a very sharp knife, cut the liver into *wafer* thin slices and then into 1$\frac{1}{2}$-inch (4-cm.) squares. Heat 1 tablespoon of oil in another pan and fry the liver briskly for just a minute on each side. Season well, add to the onions, stir well and cook together for another minute. Serve immediately with the lemon quarters.

ZUCCHINE ALLA VENEZIANA
Courgette Venetian style

A delicate vegetable dish to eat as a course on its own or to serve for a simple supper dish.

Serves 3–4

IMPERIAL/METRIC	AMERICAN
1 lb./½ kg. small courgettes	1 lb. zucchini
1 oz./25 g. butter	2 tablespoons butter
1 tablespoon oil	1 tablespoon oil
salt and pepper	salt and pepper
chopped parsley	chopped parsley
1 large egg	1 egg
1 egg yolk	1 egg yolk
grated Parmesan	grated Parmesan

Wash and dry the courgettes, cut crosswise into thin slices, discarding the ends. Heat the butter and oil in a wide heavy pan, add the courgette slices with seasoning to taste and a tablespoon of parsley. Cook over moderate heat, stirring frequently, until *just* cooked but not soft. Beat the egg, egg yolk and 1 oz. (25 g., ¼ cup) Parmesan together, add to the courgette mixture and stir continuously until the egg just begins to set. Immediately remove from the heat and serve right away so that the dish retains its delicate soft texture. Hand more grated Parmesan separately.

ARANCI CARAMELLIZZATI
Caramel oranges

This colourful dish, so popular in London's top Italian restaurants, is said to have originated in Venice using *seedless* Sicilian oranges.

Serves 4

IMPERIAL/METRIC	AMERICAN
8 large oranges	8 large oranges
8 oz./225 g. granulated sugar	1 cup sugar
water	water

Illustrated on the jacket

Pare the rind from one orange with a potato peeler. Cut it into *fine* shreds, simmer in water to cover for 5 minutes, then drain and reserve. Peel the rind, pith and white skin from *all* the oranges leaving the flesh exposed; a fine serrated knife makes the best job of this. Cut each orange crosswise into 6 slices and secure together again with a cocktail stick. Heat the sugar *gently* in ¼ pint (1½ dl., ⅔ cup) water in a small heavy saucepan until *completely dissolved*, then boil for a few minutes until cloudy and syrupy. Off the heat, lower the oranges, several at a time, into the pan and spoon the syrup over them. Remove and arrange in a serving dish. Put the reserved strips of rind into the remaining syrup and heat gently until the syrup begins to caramelise. Immediately take the pan from the heat and stand in a baking tin of warm water to stop further cooking. Quickly put some rind on top of each orange. Add ¼ pint (1½ dl., ⅔ cup) warm water to the caramel and heat and stir until the caramel dissolves. When cold, pour over the oranges. Serve chilled if possible.

GENOA AND LIGURIA

To those who seek it Liguria offers some of the most original food in Italy. The sea washing this narrow strip of Italian Riviera yields an abundance of colourful fish and shellfish. These form the basis of various fish stews, *fritto misto di mare* and antipasto, most of them quite delicious so don't be put off trying them by their unfamiliar names. Wild herbs grow rampantly on the hillsides and oregano, rosemary, sage and dill add distinctive flavours to many dishes. But *the* herb of Liguria is basil which the Genoese claim grows better there than anywhere else in Italy. This spicy aromatic herb is the basis of a unique green sauce, Pesto, which flavours and colours dishes of pasta and gnocchi, and floats on the surface of the thick Genoese version of minestrone. Spinach, mushrooms and lemons are used a great deal in Ligurian cooking. An especially aromatic variety of lemon is grown at Nervi, a town near Genoa, which is also noted for its gastronomic dinners. Olive trees flourish in many gardens and Italians take their home-grown olives to be pressed locally. This 'green' olive oil may not keep very long but it is fresh, fruity and full of flavour. No wonder the quality of olive oil is such a talking point among local cooks.

THE WINES

Liguria is not a notable wine growing area. Of the following local wines you are most likely to meet when holidaying in the area, only the Cinqueterre is exported.

White wines

Cinqueterre
Mostly dry white wines from five areas. Sciacchetra is a sweet variety.
Coronata
Usually refreshing dry white wine, good with fish.
Cortese di Liguria
Rather coarse white wine, good with fish stews.
Vermentino
Dry white wine, sometimes sparkling.

Red wines

Dolceacqua
A flavoury red wine, improves with age.

SOME FOOD SPECIALITIES

Burrida, Ciuppa or Zimmo
These are three different names for fish stews.

Capon magro
Elaborate salad of cooked vegetables and fish.
Cima
Breast of veal stuffed with minced pork, sweetbreads, pistachio nuts, peas and hard-boiled eggs. Usually eaten cold.
Fricassea di pollo
Chicken in an egg and lemon sauce.
Focaccia
Yeast pastry flavoured with sage and sometimes cheese.
Fritto allo stecco
Veal, brains, sweetbreads and mushrooms fried on a wooden skewer.
Pansotti
Stuffed pasta served with a meat sauce.
Ravioli
Famous stuffed pasta said to have originated in Liguria.
Torta Pasqualina
Easter tart of flaky pastry filled with spinach, curd cheese, artichokes, eggs and herbs.
Zuppa di datteri
Fish soup of local date-shaped shellfish.

ZUPPA DI COZZE
Mussel soup

Serves 4

IMPERIAL/METRIC	AMERICAN
1 medium onion	1 medium onion
1 stick celery	1 stalk celery
1 clove garlic	1 clove garlic
1½ lb./¾ kg. ripe tomatoes	1½ lb. ripe tomatoes
3 tablespoons olive oil	scant ¼ cup olive oil
6 tablespoons white wine	½ cup white wine
ground black pepper	ground black pepper
⅓ pint/2¼ dl. water	1 cup water
4 pints/2¼ litres fresh mussels	5 pints raw mussels
1 tablespoon chopped basil or parsley	1 tablespoon chopped basil or parsley

Prepare and finely chop the onion, celery and garlic. Skin and roughly chop the tomatoes. Heat the oil in a *large* saucepan and over gentle heat fry the onion, celery and garlic until soft. Add the wine and boil briskly until reduced by half. Add the tomatoes and pepper to taste. After another few minutes add the water, cover and simmer until the tomatoes are pulped – about 20 minutes. All this can be prepared in advance. Scrape the mussels and wash thoroughly in several changes of cold water, discarding any that do not shut tightly when touched.

Shortly before serving, heat the soup, add the mussels and cook briskly, shaking the pan frequently, until the shells open in about 10 minutes. Ladle into soup bowls and sprinkle with herbs. Serve at once with hot crusty bread.

INSALATA DI FUNGHI
Raw mushroom salad

Use very firm, small mushrooms for this refreshing meal starter.

Serves 4

IMPERIAL/METRIC	AMERICAN
1 clove garlic	1 clove garlic
6 tablespoons olive oil	½ cup olive oil
2 tablespoons lemon juice	3 tablespoons lemon juice
black pepper	black pepper
6 oz./175 g. button mushrooms	1½ cups button mushrooms
8 anchovy fillets*	8 anchovy fillets*
½ teaspoon salt	½ teaspoon salt
fresh parsley	fresh parsley

* Or 6 oz. (175 g., 1 cup) shelled prawns.

Peel the garlic, rub it around a mixing bowl then discard. In the bowl mix the oil, lemon juice and several grinds of pepper. Wipe the mushrooms, slice them very thinly and add to the bowl. Toss thoroughly with the dressing and leave in a cold place for an hour or so. Wash, dry and chop the anchovy fillets. Just before serving, add the salt to the mushrooms and toss well. Divide the mushrooms between four individual dishes, top with the anchovies (or prawns) and snip a little parsley over each.

PIZZA ALLA CASALINGA
Home-made pizza

Pizzas made at home are usually made with an enriched dough which reheats excellently, unlike the plain bread dough of a classic Neapolitan pizza. They can have a variety of fillings depending on what is available. This is a mushroom pizza with a lovely fresh flavour.

Serves 8–12

IMPERIAL/METRIC	AMERICAN
For the dough	
½ oz./15 g. fresh yeast*	½ cake compressed yeast*
little warm water	little warm water
8 oz./225 g. plain flour	2 cups all-purpose flour
1 teaspoon salt	1 teaspoon salt
2½ oz./65 g. butter	5 tablespoons butter
1 egg, beaten	1 egg, beaten
oil	oil
For the topping	
12 oz./350 g. ripe tomatoes	¾ lb. ripe tomatoes
salt and black pepper	salt and black pepper
12 oz./350 g. firm mushrooms	3 cups firm mushrooms
3–4 cloves garlic	3–4 cloves garlic
1–2 oz./25–50 g. grated Parmesan	¼–½ cup grated Parmesan

* Note If using dried yeast, dissolve 1 teaspoon sugar in 4 tablespoons warm water and sprinkle 1 level teaspoon dried yeast on top. Let it stand for 10 minutes or until frothy.

Illustrated in colour on pages 24 and 25

Blend the yeast with 4 tablespoons warm water. Sieve the flour and salt into a basin, rub in the butter and make a 'well' in the centre. Put in the egg and the blended yeast and mix to a firm but pliable dough, adding a little more water as necessary. When the dough comes cleanly away from the sides of the basin, turn it on to a floured surface and knead thoroughly for 10 minutes. Gather into a ball, put in an oiled basin, cover and leave to rise until doubled in volume – about 2–3 hours at room temperature. When risen, turn the dough on to a floured surface, divide in two and knead each piece lightly. Place in 2 well oiled 8–9-inch (20–23-cm.) aluminium pie plates and press out with floured knuckles to cover the plates and reach ½ inch (1 cm.) up the sides. Brush with oil.

While the dough is rising prepare the topping. Skin the tomatoes, squeeze out the juice and seeds. Chop the flesh, spread evenly over the two pizzas and season well. Wipe and finely slice the mushrooms, peel and chop the garlic. Heat a generous film of oil in a large frying pan and fry the mushrooms and garlic briskly (in two batches) until they give up their liquid; drain this off. Spread the mushrooms evenly over the pizzas, season well and sprinkle thickly with cheese. Bake towards the top of a preheated, hot oven (425°F., 220°C., Gas Mark 7) for 25–30 minutes.

To freeze pizza

Prepare to baking stage then wrap in heavy duty foil and freeze. Will keep frozen up to 2 months.
To reheat, remove from packaging and place frozen in a cold oven set at 450°F., 230°C., Gas Mark 8. Turn on oven and bake for 30–40 minutes.

SARDENARA
Riviera pizza

A popular pizza all along the Riviera and very different from the classic Neapolitan topping of tomatoes, cheese and anchovies. This one freezes well but add the anchovies and olives when reheating.

Serves 8–12

IMPERIAL/METRIC	AMERICAN
For the dough	
see recipe on page 39	see recipe on page 39
For the topping	
1½ lb./¾ kg. onions, peeled	1½ lb. onions, peeled
1 lb./½ kg. ripe tomatoes	1 lb. ripe tomatoes
olive oil	olive oil
salt and pepper	salt and pepper
2 oz./50 g. anchovy fillets	2 oz. anchovy fillets
few black olives	few ripe olives
dried oregano	dried oregano

Make the dough as for Pizza alla Casalinga (page 39) and line two 8-inch (20-cm.) foil pie plates. While the dough is rising, make and cool the topping. Slice the onions finely; skin and roughly chop the tomatoes. Heat 5 tablespoons of oil in a heavy pan and fry the onions gently, covered, stirring now and then until soft. This will take about 20 minutes. Add the tomatoes and seasoning and cook, uncovered, until the water has evaporated and the mixture reduced to a purée. When cold, divide between the pizzas, spread evenly, criss-cross the surface with strips of anchovy and put halves of stoned olives in the spaces. Sprinkle with oregano and oil and bake as before.

VITELLO ALL'UCCELLETTO
Sautéed veal

A very simple little dish enjoyed at a gastronomic dinner at Nervi near Genoa. My host stressed that the veal should be a good quality, the cooking speedy and the olive oil fresh and fruity.

Serves 4

IMPERIAL/METRIC	AMERICAN
1¼ lb./600 g. veal fillet	1¼ lb. veal round
olive oil	olive oil
2 cloves garlic, peeled	2 cloves garlic, peeled
3–4 bay leaves	3–4 bay leaves
salt and black pepper	salt and black pepper
4–5 tablespoons dry white wine	5–6 tablespoons dry white wine

Have the meat sliced and beaten out thinly as for veal escalopes. Cut into small pieces about the size and thickness of a 10p coin. Heat 2 tablespoons of oil with the garlic and bay leaves in a large, heavy frying pan. Off the heat, add half the veal and stir until the pieces are well lubricated with oil. Cook over brisk heat for 3 to 4 minutes, stirring frequently until the veal turns pale and is just cooked. Season and transfer to a hot serving dish. Cook the rest of the meat in the same way. Discard the garlic and bay leaves, add the wine to the frying pan and stir and heat briskly until reduced to a small amount of syrupy sauce. Spoon over the meat and serve at once with a seasonable vegetable.

SALSA GENOVESE
Veal sauce for pasta

An interesting way of making a little meat go a long way. Italian dried mushrooms are available in delicatessen stores, expensive but full of flavour; see page 7.

Serves 4

IMPERIAL/METRIC	AMERICAN
1 oz./25 g. dried mushrooms	1 oz. dried mushrooms
4 oz./100 g. lean veal	¼ lb. lean veal
2 large tomatoes	2 large tomatoes
1 oz./25 g. butter	2 tablespoons butter
4 oz./100 g. onion, chopped	1 cup chopped onion
4 oz./100 g. carrot, chopped	1 cup chopped carrot
1 stick celery, chopped	1 stalk celery, chopped
1 oz./25 g. flour	¼ cup all-purpose flour
¼ pint/1½ dl. white wine	⅔ cup white wine
½ pint/3 dl. stock	1¼ cups stock
salt and pepper	salt and pepper
grated Parmesan or Pecorino	grated Parmesan or Pecorino

Soak the mushrooms in warm water for 15 minutes. Mince or finely chop the veal. Skin and chop the tomatoes. Drain, dry and cut the mushrooms if large. Melt the butter and gently fry the onion, carrot, celery and mushrooms for 10 minutes. Add the veal, stir and cook for several minutes then add the tomatoes. Sprinkle in the flour, stir and cook for 2 minutes. Add the wine and after a few minutes the hot stock. Season, cover and simmer for at least 30 minutes.

Serve on any kind of pasta, cooked 'al dente', drained and tossed with a little olive oil. Hand grated cheese separately.

PESTO ALLA GENOVESE
Pesto sauce

Fresh basil is essential for this spicy green sauce. Although it grows anywhere with the help of a little heat, the Genoese claim their basil is superior. A proportion of parsley is permitted as it makes a greener sauce.

IMPERIAL/METRIC	AMERICAN
2 oz./50 g. fresh basil*	2 oz. fresh basil*
1 oz./25 g. pine nuts	¼ cup pine nuts
2 cloves garlic	2 cloves garlic
¼ teaspoon salt	¼ teaspoon salt
3–4 tablespoons olive oil	4–5 tablespoons olive oil
1½ oz./65 g. grated Parmesan *or* Pecorino cheese	scant ½ cup grated Parmesan *or* Pecorino cheese

* Or a mixture of basil and parsley.

Roughly chop the basil and nuts. Peel the garlic cloves. Put into a mortar with the salt and pound together until reduced to a thick paste. Add the oil little by little, stirring all the time, until the sauce acquires the consistency of whipped cream. (Alternatively put the first 4 ingredients into an electric liquidiser with 2 tablespoons of the oil and blend at slow speed, adding the remaining oil gradually until a purée is formed.) Finally stir in the cheese. Keep covered and use fresh.

TRENETTE COL PESTO
Pasta with pesto

Trenette, long strands of a narrow egg pasta, are a speciality of Genoa, but any kind of ribbon pasta can be used. Cook the pasta in the usual way, then drain thoroughly and toss with a little butter until it glistens. Serve in soup plates with a heaped spoonful of pesto on top. Before eating, thoroughly mix the pesto with the pasta and sprinkle liberally with more grated Parmesan or Pecorino cheese.

TROFFIE ALLA GENOVESE
Potato gnocchi with pesto

The pesto sauce makes this a Genoese dish. In other regions the same gnocchi are served with a meat, tomato or chicken liver sauce.

Serves 3–4

IMPERIAL/METRIC	AMERICAN
1 lb./½ kg. floury potatoes	1 lb. floury potatoes
6 oz./175 g. plain flour	1½ cups all-purpose flour
1 egg	1 egg
salt and pepper	salt and pepper
grated nutmeg	grated nutmeg
1 oz./25 g. butter	2 tablespoons butter
grated Parmesan	grated Parmesan
pesto sauce (page 41)	pesto sauce (page 41)

Peel the potatoes and boil them in salted water until tender. Drain and shake over the heat to dry them. Mash the potatoes finely, add the flour, egg and salt, pepper and nutmeg to taste; mix thoroughly. Turn on to a floured board and with floured hands roll into long sausage shapes about ½ inch (1 cm.) in diameter. Cut into 1-inch (2½-cm.) lengths and, using a little finger, make a dent in the middle of each gnocchi causing it to curl. To cook, drop the gnocchi, a few at a time, into a large pan of gently boiling, salted water. Cook for 3–5 minutes until they rise to the surface. Scoop them out with a slotted spoon, put into a buttered ovenproof dish and keep hot until all are cooked. Then dot with butter and sprinkle with cheese. Thin the pesto by stirring in a little hot water before pouring it over the gnocchi. Serve at once.

RISO ARROSTO ALLA GENOVESE
Savoury baked rice

Serves 4

IMPERIAL/METRIC	AMERICAN
1 recipe meat sauce (page 10)	1 recipe meat sauce (page 10)
1 small onion	1 small onion
4 oz./100 g. Italian sausage	¼ lb. Italian sausage
2 oz./50 g. mushrooms	½ cup mushrooms
1½ oz./40 g. butter	3 tablespoons butter
5 oz./150 g. shelled peas	1 cup shelled peas
8 oz./225 g. Italian rice	generous 1 cup Italian rice
1½ oz./40 g. grated Parmesan	scant ½ cup grated Parmesan
¼ pint/1½ dl. stock	⅔ cup stock

Make the meat sauce. Peel and chop the onion, skin and chop the sausage, wipe and slice the mushrooms. Preheat a moderate oven (350°F., 180°C., Gas Mark 4). Melt the butter and fry the onion and sausage gently for 5 minutes. Add the mushrooms and peas, and stir and cook for a few minutes. In another pan, cook the rice in boiling, salted water for 5 minutes then drain and add to the onion mixture. Stir in the meat sauce, cheese and stock. Transfer to a greased ovenproof dish. Cook, uncovered, in the centre of the oven until the liquid is absorbed, the rice tender and a thick golden crust forms over the surface of the dish. This takes from 30–40 minutes.

FUNGHI FRESCHI AL FUNGHETTO
Fried mushrooms

A typical Ligurian dish of mushrooms – fresh tasting and enlivened with herbs and garlic.

Wash and dry the amount of mushrooms needed and cut into dice. Heat some oil in a frying pan, add the mushrooms and season with salt, ground black pepper and a little nutmeg. Fry over brisk heat until the moisture has evaporated. Lower the heat and add a little very finely chopped oregano (or marjoram) and garlic to taste. Stir around and serve immediately with crisp toast.

BOLOGNA, EMILIA-ROMAGNA

Emilia-Romagna with Bologna as the centre is a 'must' for everyone seriously interested in good eating. This region produces many famous specialities and the convivial inhabitants really care about food. Pork products predominate with hams and sausages of all kinds including mortadella, the salami of Felino, zampone – a pig's foot stuffed with minced spiced pork, and its smaller relative, cotechino. The lovely town of Parma is the centre of the district producing the delicately cured Parma ham, eaten raw in wafer thin slices and often served with ripe melon or figs. The area between Parma and Modena is Parmesan cheese country, the cheese whose piquant flavour has done more to popularise Italian cooking abroad than any other single food. Local inhabitants consider their pasta unbeatable, and in Bologna it is 'tagliatelle', a ribbon pasta, they serve with the legendary Bolognese meat sauce and *not* spaghetti. The sauce itself is made with loving care and is much richer than the ordinary '*salsa*' or '*sugo di carne*' found elsewhere. For special occasions stuffed pasta, such as tortellini filled with a rich mixture of minced pork, veal and poultry, are still made in the home – every town claims to have the 'best' recipe!

At coastal towns such as Ravenna, Rimini and Riccione, another 'must' is a visit to the harbour restaurants serving their own colourful '*brodetto*' (fish stew) and barbecued fresh sardines and scampi. Excellent vegetables, cherries and eels are all produced in Emilia-Romagna, not to mention the wine to wash it down. At a farm house dinner near Riccione, where everything including the wine was home made, our genial host deliberately dropped a tray of crockery – not by accident but as a dramatic protest that one of the guests had dared to ask for water!

THE WINES

In contrast to the rich food of this region, the wines are relatively light. But, as the natives are quick to point out, they have an uncanny way of being happy partners for the local dishes. And so it proves to be when put to the test.

White wines

Albana
A light gold to amber coloured wine, mellow and medium sweet. There is also a sweet Albana.

Red wines

Lambrusco wines
These are unusual wines, dry and semi-sparkling, which froth as they are poured out and leave a definite 'prickle' on the tongue. They are found in practically every restaurant and the Lambrusco di Sorbara is considered the best. The locals recommend it for drinking with zampone, cotechino and stuffed pastas.

Sangiovese
A dry red wine, said to improve with age.

SOME FOOD SPECIALITIES

Anguille
Eels, the best come from Comacchio.

Anolini, Cappelletti and Tortellini
The names of three different stuffed pastas.

Bomba di riso
Rice and pigeon dish from Parma.

Brodetto
Colourful fish stew.

Cotechino
Large raw sausage stuffed with spiced pork.

Culatello di zibello
Cured loin of pork eaten like ham.

Involtini
Thin slice veal rolled around various stuffings and braised.

Mortadella
Very large cooked sausage.
Porcini
Edible fungi, often dried.
Riso con l'anitra
Rice with duck and giblet sauce.
Tortelli d'erbette
Pasta stuffed with cheese and spinach.
Zampone
Pig's foot stuffed with raw spiced pork.

CHEESES

Grana
Generic name for all fine grained cheeses of the Parmesan type.
Parmigiano
The famous grating and cooking cheese (page 6). When *fresh*, Parmesan is also a delicious table cheese.

PASSATELLI IN BRODO
Cheese noodles in broth

An unusual soup, light and nourishing, very suitable for invalids and young children.

Serves 3–4

IMPERIAL/METRIC	AMERICAN
1½ pints/scant 1 litre chicken broth	3¾ cups chicken broth
1 oz./25 g. grated Parmesan	¼ cup grated Parmesan
1 egg	1 egg
2 teaspoons flour	2 teaspoons flour
½ tablespoon butter	½ tablespoon butter
1 oz./25 g. fine soft breadcrumbs	½ cup fine soft bread crumbs
salt and pepper	salt and pepper

In a wide saucepan bring the broth to the boil. Put the cheese, egg, flour, butter and 2 level tablespoons of the breadcrumbs into a basin and work to a stiff paste with a wooden spoon. If necessary add a few more breadcrumbs. Press the pasta through the coarse holes of a colander into the boiling soup. In 1–2 minutes, when the worm-like noodles rise to the surface, remove the pan from the heat and leave to stand for 5 minutes. Season if necessary before serving.

FRITTO MISTO ALL'EMILIANA
Mixed fry Emilia style

The ingredients of a '*fritto misto*' vary according to the region, the season and the contents of the larder. Unless it is specifically a '*fritto misto mare*' (fish) or '*fritto misto verdure*' (vegetables), it should contain a mixture of vegetables and meats, all tender and cut in small pieces.

Serves 4

IMPERIAL/METRIC	AMERICAN
1 aubergine	1 eggplant
salt	salt
frying batter (page 11)	frying batter (page 11)
8 oz./225 g. veal sweetbread or thin pieces veal	½ lb. veal sweetbreads or thin pieces veal
8 cauliflower flowerets	8 cauliflower florets
4 pieces calf's liver	4 pieces calf's liver
2 courgettes, sliced	2 zucchini, sliced
oil for frying	oil for frying
To garnish	
1 lemon, quartered	1 lemon, quartered
sprigs parsley	sprigs parsley

Cut the aubergine in ¼-inch (½-cm.) thick slices, sprinkle with salt and leave to drain in a colander for an hour. Then rinse and pat dry. Mix the batter, leaving just the egg white to whisk stiffly and fold in just before using. Clean and blanch the sweetbread and cut into 4 pieces. Cook the cauliflower in salted water for 2 minutes only. When ready to fry, heat pan of oil to 375°F., 190°C. (cube of bread should turn golden in about 45 seconds). Starting with the foods that need longest to cook, dry the pieces if necessary and sprinkle lightly with salt. Dip each piece in batter then lower gently into the fat and fry until golden and cooked. Fry in batches, allowing the fat to regain frying temperature before cooking the next batch. As the foods are cooked, drain carefully on crumpled paper and keep hot. When all are ready, arrange in groups on a large hot plate and garnish with lemon wedges and sprigs of parsley. Serve immediately.

RAGÙ BOLOGNESE
Bolognese meat sauce

A real Bolognese sauce is, and should be, a rich sauce. For a plainer, everyday meat sauce, see *Salsi di Carne*, page 10. Both sauces freeze well. In Bologna you won't find their famous sauce served on spaghetti, but always with the more delicate ribbon pasta known as tagliatelle. In Rome the same pasta is called fettuccine.

Serves 4 (with pasta)

IMPERIAL/METRIC	AMERICAN	
1 medium onion	1 medium onion	Prepare and finely chop the onion, carrot, celery and bacon. Put into a saucepan with the butter and fry together very gently until tender and golden – about 10 minutes. Add the meat and stir and brown lightly, then add the wine and allow to bubble briskly until almost evaporated. Stir in the stock and tomato purée, with salt, pepper and nutmeg to taste. Cover and simmer *very gently* for at least 45 minutes, stirring now and then. Lastly, stir in the cream or butter and check the seasoning.
1 medium carrot	1 medium carrot	
1 stick celery	1 stalk celery	
2 oz./50 g. streaky bacon	3 bacon slices	
½ oz./15 g. butter	1 tablespoon butter	
8 oz./225 g. raw minced beef	1 cup firmly packed raw ground beef	
4 tablespoons white wine	⅓ cup white wine	
½ pint/3 dl. stock or water	1¼ cups stock or water	
1 tablespoon tomato purée	1 tablespoon tomato paste	
salt and black pepper	salt and black pepper	
grated nutmeg	grated nutmeg	
2 tablespoons thick cream *or* 1 oz./25 g. butter	3 tablespoons whipping cream *or* 2 tablespoons butter	

TAGLIATELLE ALLA BOLOGNESE
Ribbon pasta with meat sauce

Serves 4

IMPERIAL/METRIC	AMERICAN	
ragù Bolognese (above)	ragù Bolognese (above)	Make the sauce allowing time for it to cook very slowly. Fifteen minutes before serving, cook the tagliatelle in plenty of boiling, salted water until just tender but still 'al dente'. Drain thoroughly and put into a heated serving dish with the butter. Add about 2 tablespoons of sauce and one of cheese and toss lightly with 2 forks until the pasta is well coated. Serve the remaining sauce on top and hand more grated Parmesan separately.
12 oz./350 g. tagliatelle	¾ lb. tagliatelle	
1–2 oz./25–50 g. butter	2–4 tablespoons butter	
grated Parmesan	grated Parmesan	

TAGLIATELLE VERDI CON PROSCIUTTO
Green ribbon pasta with ham

Serves 4

Chop 4 oz. (100 g.) lean sliced gammon and fry very gently for 5 minutes in 2 oz. (50 g., ¼ cup) butter. Pour over 12 oz. (350 g.) green tagliatelle freshly cooked 'al dente', sprinkle with 2 heaped tablespoons grated Parmesan, toss lightly together and serve at once.

LASAGNE AL FORNO
Baked lasagne

This popular dish should be moist and creamy with a bubbling golden top. It freezes and reheats very successfully.

Serves 4

IMPERIAL/METRIC	AMERICAN
1 recipe ragù Bolognese (page 45)	1 recipe ragù Bolognese (page 45)
4 oz./100 g. wide lasagne*	¼ lb. wide lasagne*
1 recipe béchamel sauce (page 9)	1 recipe béchamel sauce (page 9)
3 tablespoons thick cream	scant ¼ cup whipping cream
2 oz./50 g. grated Parmesan	½ cup grated Parmesan

* White or verdi (green), as you please.

Prepare the meat sauce in advance. Cook the lasagne in plenty of fast boiling, salted water following the label directions. Drain carefully and lay the lasagne flat on a clean tea cloth. Meanwhile make the béchamel sauce and, when cooked, stir in the cream. Butter an ovenproof dish about 8 × 6 × 2 inches deep (20 × 15 × 5 cm.). Arrange alternate layers of meat sauce, overlapping strips of pasta, béchamel and a sprinkling of Parmesan. Finish with a smooth layer of béchamel and a thick coating of cheese. Bake in a moderate oven (350°F., 180°C., Gas Mark 4) for 25–30 minutes, for the pasta to absorb the flavours and for the top to brown. Cut in squares to serve.

SPIEDINI DI SCAMPI
Barbecued scampi on skewers

Along the coast jetty-side, restaurants prepare barbecued fresh scampi 'just as the sailors do at sea'. We can do the same in the back garden though it is doubtful if the scampi will taste as good. In Riccione skewers are made from Tamerisk twigs.

IMPERIAL/METRIC	AMERICAN
raw peeled scampi*	raw peeled jumbo shrimp*
beaten egg	beaten egg
dry white breadcrumbs	dried white bread crumbs
pepper	pepper
quartered lemon	quartered lemon

* Barely thawed frozen scampi, preferably large ones, well drained and dried. Allow about 4 oz. (100 g.) per person.

Fill a large shallow tin tray with sand and make a small charcoal fire in the centre of it. Coat the scampi with egg and breadcrumbs, patting the coating on firmly. Impale securely on skewers keeping the scampi at the pointed end and covering only half the length of the skewer. Sprinkle scampi with pepper. When the fire is glowing, stick the empty end of the skewer into the sand leaving the pointed end containing the scampi over the fire. Grill until golden, turning once, for about 5 minutes. Serve on the skewer, with a quarter of lemon to squeeze over them.

COSTELETTE DI VITELLO ALLA MODENESE
Veal escalope with ham and cheese

Slices of chicken or turkey breasts are good cooked this way too.

Serves 4

IMPERIAL/METRIC	AMERICAN
4 thin escalopes veal	4 thin scallops veal
little seasoned flour	little seasoned flour
1 egg, beaten	1 egg, beaten
fine white breadcrumbs	fine white bread crumbs
about 2 oz./50 g. butter	about ¼ cup butter
4 thin slices ham	4 thin slices cured ham
4 thin slices cheese*	4 thin slices cheese*

* Fontina, Bel Paese or any good 'melting' cheese.

Beat the veal out very thinly. Coat each slice with seasoned flour then with egg and finally breadcrumbs, pressing the coating on firmly. Melt the butter in a large frying pan and fry the escalopes gently until golden – about 3 minutes each side. Arrange flat on a flameproof serving dish, lay a similar size slice of ham on top of each and top that with a slice of cheese. Slip the escalopes under a hot grill until the cheese is melting and golden.

FILETTI DI TACCHINO BOLOGNESE
Turkey breasts with ham and cheese

Turkey breast meat can be bought frozen or chilled nowadays, this is a good way of cooking it.

Serves 4

IMPERIAL/METRIC	AMERICAN
1 lb./½ kg. turkey breasts	1 lb. turkey breasts
salt and pepper	salt and pepper
flour	flour
butter	butter
olive oil	olive oil
4 oz./100 g. sliced ham*	¼ lb. sliced cured ham*
grated Parmesan	grated Parmesan
¼ pint/1½ dl. chicken stock	⅔ cup chicken stock
* Either prosciutto or cooked ham.	

Cut the turkey meat into 8 slices, place between greaseproof paper and flatten each slice with a rolling pin. Dust them with salt, pepper and flour. Heat 1 oz. (25 g., 2 tablespoons) butter and 1 tablespoon of oil in a heavy frying pan and fry the fillets (only 4 at a time as they must be flat; or use 2 pans) gently for 10 minutes, turning once. Lay a similar size slice of ham on each fillet and cover with a generous layer of Parmesan. Pour a tablespoonful of stock over each, cover the pan and cook very gently for another 10 minutes or transfer to a moderate oven for 15 minutes. Serve at once with buttered courgettes or French beans.

FINOCCHIO ALLA PARMIGIANA
Fennel baked with cheese

The gentle anise flavour of cooked fennel is delicious eaten on its own or with veal or chicken dishes.

Serves 3

IMPERIAL/METRIC	AMERICAN
1 lb./½ kg. fennel bulbs	1 lb. fennel bulbs
2 tablespoons milk	3 tablespoons milk
1 oz./25 g. grated Parmesan	¼ cup grated Parmesan
1½ oz./40 g. butter	3 tablespoons butter

Preheat a moderately hot oven (400°F., 200°C., Gas Mark 6). Remove the coarse outer leaves and cook the fennel in boiling, salted water for 15 minutes. Drain. Cut vertically into 3 or 4 slices. Arrange these flat in a well buttered shallow ovenproof dish. Pour the milk over, sprinkle thickly with cheese and dot with butter. Cook, uncovered, towards the top of the oven until tender and golden – about 20–30 minutes.

CAVOLFIORE ALLA ROMAGNOLA
Cauliflower Romagna style

Serves 4

IMPERIAL/METRIC	AMERICAN
1 cauliflower	1 cauliflower
1 oz./25 g. butter	2 tablespoons butter
3 tablespoons olive oil	scant ¼ cup olive oil
1 clove garlic, crushed	1 clove garlic, crushed
chopped parsley	chopped parsley
salt and pepper	salt and pepper
1 tablespoon tomato purée	1 tablespoon tomato paste
6 tablespoons hot water	½ cup hot water
grated Parmesan	grated Parmesan

Divide the cauliflower into individual flowerets, wash and drain. Heat the butter and oil in a saucepan and fry the garlic and parsley for a few moments. Add the cauliflower, stir and cook for several minutes then add salt and pepper, and tomato purée mixed with the water. Cover the pan and cook over *low* heat until tender – from 5–10 minutes. Turn into a serving dish, sprinkle with cheese and serve hot.

FLORENCE AND TUSCANY

Tuscan cooking is renowned for its simplicity. The regional recipes have grown up around locally produced ingredients of a quality that needs neither elaborate sauces nor extravagant garnishes. Although beef, beans and Chianti are the first products to spring to mind, the gentle Tuscan countryside yields an abundance of grain, vegetables of all kinds and fruit. Hares, game and small birds are much in evidence, the latter often seen spit roasting in local restaurants. Arezzo is famous for its hams, pork and cherries. Chicken dishes are especially good in Tuscany and they use chicken livers and giblets to advantage (see Chicken liver savouries, page 58). Lucca produces the finest olive oil in Italy and the local cooking is at its best in early autumn when the new season's olives are pressed. Fresh herbs are a feature in the markets and are used freely in Tuscan cooking. On the coast, Leghorn boasts a famous fish soup, while further south a variety of eel is the speciality; and at Pisa, tiny, still blind, eel-fry are caught in the silted up river Arno. So, when in Tuscany leave the overlarge 'bistecca alla fiorentina' to the gluttonous and seek out some of the more original dishes.

THE WINES

Although Tuscany is the home of Chianti, the best known of all Italian red wines, it also produces many good white wines. The Wine Library of Italy, the Enotoca, housed in an old Medici castle at Siena, is well worth a visit.

Red wines

Chianti Classico
Famous dry wine produced within legally defined limits around Florence and Siena. Only wine produced within this area may carry the sign of authenticity – a black cockerel on a gold background.
Other Chiantis
Neighbouring vineyards outside the defined area produce good if lesser wines of similar type e.g. Chianti Montalbano.
Vino Nobile di Montepulciano
A fine 'big' wine which needs at least five years bottle age.
Alecatico
Sweetish red wine from Elba. Drink between meals or with puddings.
Brunello di Montalcino
Full bodied wine, very long lived.

White wines

Arbia
Light dry white wine.
Procanico Elbano
Well known dry wine from Elba. Good with fish.
Moscato dell'Elba
Sweet white wine for desserts.
Vernaccia di San Gimignano
Dry white wine from the Siennese hills.
Vino Santo Toscano
Widely produced sweet white wine which needs 3 to 4 years bottle age.

SOME FOOD SPECIALITIES

Bistecca alla fiorentina or Costata alla fiorentina
Huge T bone steak, grilled.
Bruschetta
Crisp baked bread slices rubbed with garlic and doused with new olive oil.
Cacciucco alla livornese
Spicy fish stew containing red wine and some shellfish.
Capitone
Large eel.

Salad of artichoke hearts (page 73)

Cée or Ceche
Tiny eel-fry cooked with oil, sage, lemon and garlic.
Fagioli al fiasco
Traditional way of cooking white beans with oil and seasoning in a glass flask.
Fegatini di maiale
Squares of pigs' liver, bread and bay leaves cooked on a spit.
Finocchiona
Spicy salami flavoured with fennel seeds.
Fritto misto fiorentina
Pieces of chicken, brains, sweetbreads, artichoke hearts and Mozzarella all battered and deep fried.

Minestrone di fagioli
Thick mixed vegetable soup containing beans.
Tortino di carciofi
Flat omelette containing sliced artichokes.
Triglie alla livornese
Fried mullet in tomato sauce.
Uccelletti
Small birds such as larks, thrushes and quails usually spit roasted or grilled.

FAGIOLI CON TONNO
Beans with tunny fish

An antipasto made locally from fresh Tuscan beans but dried or canned beans can be used. Good olive oil is important.
Serves 4

IMPERIAL/METRIC	AMERICAN
6 oz./175 g. dried white beans	generous 1 cup navy beans
about 2 oz. onion, coarsely grated	½ cup coarsely grated onion
olive oil	olive oil
salt and black pepper	salt and black pepper
1 (8 oz./225 g.) can tunny fish	1 (8 oz.) can tuna fish

Soak the beans overnight in water to cover. Drain, cover with fresh water and simmer for 2–3 hours, until tender. Drain the beans and whilst still hot, mix with the coarsely grated onion, a liberal dressing of olive oil and seasoning to taste. When cold, serve in shallow bowls topped with a large chunk of tunny fish.

PAPPARDELLE CON LA LEPRE
Pasta with hare sauce

Pappardelle are wide strips of pasta, but any ribbon pasta will do. The hare sauce is rich and tasty and can be made from the legs when a saddle of hare has been roasted. It freezes well.
Serves 4

IMPERIAL/METRIC	AMERICAN
1 lb./½ kg. hare joints	1 lb. hare pieces
3 oz./75 g. onion	3 oz. onion
3 oz./75 g. carrot	3 oz. carrot
1 stick celery	1 stalk celery
1 clove garlic	1 clove garlic
3 oz./75 g. unsmoked bacon	3 oz. unsmoked bacon
1 oz./25 g. lard	2 tablespoons lard
salt and pepper	salt and pepper
½ teaspoon dried thyme	½ teaspoon dried thyme
2 tablespoons flour	3 tablespoons flour
6 tablespoons red wine	½ cup red wine
½ pint/3 dl. water	1¼ cups water
1 teaspoon lemon juice	1 teaspoon lemon juice
10–12 oz./275–350 g. pappardelle	about ¾ lb. pappardelle
grated Parmesan	grated Parmesan

Strip the meat from the hare bones and cut into fine strips, removing all sinews. This needs patience but the sauce is worth it. Prepare all the vegetables and chop finely. Cut the bacon into strips. Melt the lard in a saucepan and gently fry the bacon and vegetables together until soft and golden, stirring from time to time. Add the hare, seasoning and herb, stir and cook for several minutes before stirring in the flour and cooking for another 2 minutes. Add the wine and allow to boil for a few minutes, then add the water. Cover tightly and simmer for about 1 hour, stirring occasionally, until cooked and reduced to a thick rich sauce. Add the lemon juice and check the seasoning.

Cook the pasta in plenty of fast boiling, salted water until tender but 'al dente'. Drain thoroughly, put into a hot serving dish and stir in 2 tablespoons of grated Parmesan. Serve the hare sauce separately.

GNOCCHI VERDI
Spinach gnocchi

These pretty green gnocchi make a light and attractive luncheon dish. They don't freeze well, but can be prepared ahead and kept in a domestic refrigerator until later the same day.

Serves 4

IMPERIAL/METRIC	AMERICAN
1 (8 oz./225 g.) carton frozen chopped spinach	1 (½ lb.) carton frozen chopped spinach
8 oz./225 g. Ricotta*	½ lb. Ricotta*
salt and pepper	salt and pepper
grated nutmeg	grated nutmeg
½ oz./15 g. butter	1 tablespoon butter
2 eggs	2 eggs
1½ oz./40 g. grated Parmesan	scant ½ cup grated Parmesan
2 oz./50 g. plain flour	½ cup all-purpose flour
To finish	
2 oz./50 g. butter	¼ cup butter
1 oz./25 g. grated Parmesan	¼ cup grated Parmesan
* Or curd cheese.	

Put the spinach, frozen or thawed, into a small saucepan and place over *low* heat. Cook very gently until *completely* thawed then increase the heat and cook, stirring frequently, until all the moisture has evaporated and the spinach is really dry. This is essential otherwise the mixture will be too soft. Add the Ricotta, liberal seasonings of salt, pepper and nutmeg, and the butter. Stir together over the heat for several minutes. Off the heat, beat in the eggs, Parmesan and flour, mixing thoroughly. Set aside in a cold place until firm. To shape, take a tablespoonful of mixture at a time and with well floured hands roll into ping pong size balls. To cook, lower the balls, a few at a time, into a pan of gently simmering, salted water. When they rise to the top, in 4 to 5 minutes, they are ready. Immediately remove with a slotted spoon and drain on kitchen paper. Transfer to a shallow flameproof dish and keep warm. When all the gnocchi are cooked, heat the 2 oz. (50 g.) butter until pale brown then pour over the gnocchi and sprinkle with grated Parmesan. Serve immediately.

Illustrated in colour on page 53

UOVA IN UMIDO ALLA FIORENTINA
Eggs – Florentine style

This is a substantial main course or picnic dish. Italians use prosciutto or pancetta for the ham, but we can use very thinly sliced gammon or unsmoked bacon.

Serves 4

IMPERIAL/METRIC	AMERICAN
4 thin slices leg veal	4 thin slices veal round
4 slices raw ham	4 slices raw cured ham or unsmoked bacon
4 hard-boiled eggs	4 hard-cooked eggs
1 tablespoon oil	1 tablespoon oil
1 oz./25 g. butter	2 tablespoons butter
1 sprig rosemary	1 sprig rosemary
4 tablespoons white wine	⅓ cup white wine
1 tablespoon tomato purée	1 tablespoon tomato paste
5 tablespoons boiling water	6 tablespoons boiling water
sugar	sugar
salt and pepper	salt and pepper

Beat each piece of meat with a rolling pin until large and thin enough to completely envelop an egg. Lay flat, cover with a piece of ham and put a shelled egg in the centre of each. Wrap the meat around the eggs, folding neatly over each end securing with white cotton wound around. Heat the oil, butter and rosemary in a heavy pan and fry the rolls until lightly browned all over. Add the wine and bubble briskly until well reduced. Mix the tomato purée with the boiling water and add to the pan with seasonings of sugar, salt and pepper. Cover tightly and simmer very gently for about 1 hour, turning the rolls once, adding a little more water should the liquid evaporate too much. Serve hot or cold.

Rabbit with green olives (page 77)

Spinach gnocchi (page 51)

ARISTÀ FIORENTINA
Florentine roast pork

Pork cooked in this way is excellent for serving cold – moist, tender and deliciously flavoured.

Serves 7–9

IMPERIAL/METRIC	AMERICAN
3 lb./1½ kg. loin of pork	3 lb. loin roast of pork
2 cloves garlic	2 cloves garlic
fresh rosemary	fresh rosemary
salt	salt
ground black pepper	ground black pepper

Preheat a moderate oven (350°F., 180°C., Gas Mark 4). Remove the rind from the pork. Peel the garlic and cut into slithers. With a pointed knife, make deep incisions in the meat and press a slither of garlic and a spike of rosemary into each. Rub the meat generously with salt and pepper. Place on a trivet standing in a roasting tin containing 1 inch (2½ cm.) of water. Cook in the centre of the oven for 45 minutes per 1 lb. (½ kg.) of weight, until cooked through and golden. May be eaten hot, but this pork dish is usually served cold garlanded with sprigs of fresh rosemary.

SCALOPPINE DI VITELLIO AL MARSALA
Escalopes of veal with Marsala

Serves 4

IMPERIAL/METRIC	AMERICAN
8 small veal escalopes, about 1½ oz./40 g. each	8 small veal scallops, about 1½ oz. each
½ lemon	½ lemon
salt and pepper	salt and pepper
little flour	little flour
2 oz./50 g. butter	¼ cup butter
2 tablespoons oil	3 tablespoons oil
2 tablespoons chicken stock	3 tablespoons chicken stock
3 tablespoons Marsala	scant ¼ cup Marsala
little chopped parsley	little chopped parsley

With a rolling pin, beat out each piece of veal as thinly as possible. Rub them over with the cut lemon, squeezing lightly to release the juice. Sprinkle with salt and pepper and dust with flour. Heat the butter and oil in a large frying pan and when hot brown the veal quickly on each side (you may have to do this in two batches). Lower the heat, add the chicken stock and continue cooking gently for 5 minutes. Arrange the veal on a serving dish and keep warm. Add the Marsala to the buttery juices in the pan and boil briskly for a minute or so until syrupy. Pour over the veal and sprinkle lightly with parsley.

MAIALE UBRIACO
Intoxicated pork chops

By the time these chops are cooked they have absorbed or 'drunk' most of the wine – hence the name. The wine used in Tuscany is a young Chianti but any light dry wine is suitable.

Serves 4

IMPERIAL/METRIC	AMERICAN
4 lean pork chops	4 lean pork chops
salt and black pepper	salt and black pepper
2 tablespoons olive oil	3 tablespoons olive oil
2 cloves garlic, crushed	2 cloves garlic, crushed
about ½ pint/3 dl. red wine	about 1¼ cups red wine
To garnish	
chopped fresh parsley	chopped fresh parsley
1 lemon, quartered	1 lemon, quartered

Season the chops with salt and pepper. Heat the oil and garlic in a wide pan and fry the chops in a single layer until lightly browned each side. Add wine just to cover the chops, put a lid on the pan and simmer gently until the meat has absorbed most of the wine – about 30 minutes. Place the chops in a serving dish, pour the remaining wine over them and sprinkle with parsley. Garnish with lemon. Serve with a crisp green salad and fluffy creamed potato.

POLLO ALLA DIAVOLA
Grilled marinated chicken

This method of marinating in oil and lemon juice is a good way of adding flavour to chicken. Chicken joints, marinated then floured, egg and crumbed and deep fried become *Pollo fritto alla fiorentina*.

Serves 2

IMPERIAL/METRIC	AMERICAN
2 chicken halves, about 1 lb./½ kg. each	2 chicken halves, about 1 lb. each
3 tablespoons olive oil	scant ¼ cup olive oil
1½ tablespoons lemon juice	2 tablespoons lemon juice
1 clove garlic, crushed	1 clove garlic, crushed
1 bay leaf, crumbled	1 bay leaf, crumbled
¼ teaspoon rosemary	¼ teaspoon rosemary
little chopped parsley	little chopped parsley
1 teaspoon salt	1 teaspoon salt
½ teaspoon ground black pepper	½ teaspoon ground black pepper

Wash and dry the chicken halves and place flat in a shallow dish. Mix all the remaining ingredients together and pour over the chicken. Leave to marinate for 2–3 hours, turning once. To cook, place the chicken skin side down on a grill rack and cook under medium heat, 5 to 6 inches (13 to 15 cm.) below the grill, for 10 minutes. Turn skin side up and continue cooking, basting frequently with the marinade, for another 12–15 minutes, or until golden and cooked. Serve with a green salad and sauté potatoes.

LINGUA IN SALSA AGRODOLCE
Tongue in sweet-sour sauce

A lightly salted, home cooked tongue is the best and most economical basis for this recipe. Otherwise use bought tongue sliced fairly thickly.

Serves 4

IMPERIAL/METRIC	AMERICAN
1¼ lb./600 g. cooked ox tongue	1¼ lb. cooked ox or beef tongue
For the sauce	
2 oz./50 g. onion, chopped	½ cup chopped onion
2 tablespoons oil	3 tablespoons oil
1 oz./25 g. flour	¼ cup all-purpose flour
¾ pint/4½ dl. meat stock	2 cups meat stock
2 tablespoons wine vinegar	3 tablespoons wine vinegar
2 tablespoons brown sugar	3 tablespoons brown sugar
1 tablespoon sultanas	1 tablespoon seedless white raisins
1 tablespoon pine nuts	1 tablespoon pine nuts
grated rind ½ orange	grated rind ½ orange
pinch ground cloves	pinch ground cloves

Make the sauce in advance as follows. Fry the onion *gently* in the oil until beginning to soften, then stir in the flour and cook over very low heat until pale fawn, stirring frequently. Add the hot stock and whisk briskly until boiling and blended to a smooth sauce. Add all the other ingredients, stir well, cover and simmer for 30 minutes. Arrange the tongue in overlapping slices in an ovenproof dish and pour the sauce over them. Cover and leave in a moderate to low oven for 20–30 minutes, so that the meat becomes impregnated with the sauce. Serve with a seasonable vegetable.

Spaghetti with bacon, pepper and tomatoes (page 63)

Lemon water ice (page 78)

TRIPPA ALLA TOSCANA
Tripe – Tuscany style

A simple but good and colourful way of cooking tripe. Mint is often used instead of marjoram.

Serves 4

IMPERIAL/METRIC	AMERICAN
1 lb./½ kg. veal tripe	1 lb. veal tripe
salt	salt
1 small onion	1 small onion
1 stick celery	1 stalk celery
1 recipe tomato sauce	1 recipe tomato sauce
(page 9)	(page 9)
1 teaspoon marjoram	1 teaspoon marjoram
grated Parmesan	grated Parmesan

Simmer the tripe in salted water to which the sliced onion and celery have been added. When *just* tender – this will take about 1 hour but start testing after 45 minutes to avoid overcooking – cut into 2 inch (5 cm.) wide strips. Put these into a buttered flameproof dish with the tomato sauce and the finely chopped marjoram. Heat gently over a low flame for 10 minutes. Sprinkle thickly with Parmesan before serving and hand more cheese separately.

CROSTINI ALLA FIORENTINA
Chicken liver savouries

An excellent meal starter or savoury. The sage flavour is important, but use sparingly.

Serves 4

IMPERIAL/METRIC	AMERICAN
8 oz./225 g. chicken livers	½ lb. chicken livers
1 oz./25 g. shallot	1 oz. shallot
1½ oz./40 g. butter	3 tablespoons butter
3 fresh sage leaves	3 fresh sage leaves
ground black pepper	ground black pepper
1 teaspoon lemon juice	1 teaspoon lemon juice
8 slices French bread*	8 slices French bread*
butter for frying	butter for frying
little chopped parsley	little chopped parsley
* Cut slant-wise from a small French loaf.	

Wash the livers, discarding any tissues, and chop finely. Finely chop the shallot. Melt the butter in a small pan and gently cook the shallot and sage leaves together for 5 minutes. Discard the sage. Add the livers and a few grinds of pepper. Cook gently, stirring frequently, until no pink colour remains – about 6–7 minutes. Stir in the lemon juice. Meanwhile fry the bread quickly in butter until golden each side. Spread each with the liver mixture and sprinkle with parsley. Serve immediately, two for each person.

BUDINO DI RICOTTA
Ricotta pudding

Serves 4

IMPERIAL/METRIC	AMERICAN
dry white breadcrumbs	dried white bread crumbs
8 oz./225 g. Ricotta cheese*	½ lb. Ricotta cheese*
1½ oz./40 g. candied orange peel	¼ cup candied orange peel
3 egg yolks	3 egg yolks
3 oz./75 g. castor sugar	6 tablespoons sugar
2 oz./50 g. ground almonds	½ cup ground almonds
1½ oz./40 g. sultanas	¼ cup seedless white raisins
1 teaspoon grated lemon rind	1 teaspoon grated lemon rind
little icing sugar	little confectioners' sugar
*Or curd cheese or home-made cream cheese (page 6).	

Preheat a moderate oven (350°F., 180°C., Gas Mark 4). Butter a 6-inch (15-cm.) diameter false bottomed tin and coat with breadcrumbs. Press the cheese through a sieve and chop the candied peel finely. In a mixing bowl, beat the egg yolks and sugar together until light, then beat in the cheese, candied peel, almonds, sultanas and lemon rind. Transfer to the prepared tin, smooth the surface and sprinkle with breadcrumbs. Cook in the centre of the oven until firm to the touch – about 30 minutes. Leave in the tin until quite cold, then remove and dust with sugar. Serve cut in wedges.

ROME AND LAZIO

If you want to try the robust dishes typical of this region, you must eat where the Romans eat rather than in tourist hotels and restaurants. Look for the family 'trattorie' and 'osteria' patronised by the locals and where the dishes offered will be mainly of foods in season. In spring don't miss the young tender artichokes which are fried and flattened in a manner found nowhere else (*carciofi alla guida*). The variety and quality of vegetables piled high on the market stalls is spectacular, and the ways of cooking them often original. Rome has adopted as her own many dishes from other parts of Italy; it is the place where the ribbon pasta of the North and the tubular pasta of the South meet. The sauces served with pasta are often robust and sometimes peppery. Hearty dishes of cannelloni with various fillings are popular. Dishes of baby lamb (*abbacchio*) and roasted, herb stuffed suckling pig (*porchetta*) are characteristic. The Latina coast has excellent fish, especially spiny lobsters and giant prawns. And the fisherman can cook too, for when I helped judge a competition to find Italy's best fish soup it was a boatcrew from Anzio who won it!

THE WINES

Most of the wines you find in Lazio are produced locally either in the castle villages of the Alban hills (the Castelli Romani) or around Lake Bolsena. Most are dryish light wines but order carefully as many have medium dry or sweet versions also. Orvieto, a popular wine outside Italy, is not a Roman wine but comes from neighbouring Umbria.

White wines

Colli Albani
Light golden dry wine. There is also a sweet version.
Colli Lanuvi
As above.
Est! Est! Est!
Dry or semi-dry, and light.
Frascati
Dry or semi-sweet light golden wine.
Moscato
Sweet, rich dessert wine.
Orvieto
Well known dry white wine (*secco*), but there is also a semi-sweet variety (*abboccato*).

Red wines

Cecubo
Pale red wine, said to be the wine that Cicero drank!
Cesanese
Dry or sweet red wine, sometimes '*frizzante*'.
Velletri
Light, dry red wine.

SOME FOOD SPECIALITIES

Abbacchio
Baby lamb cooked in various ways, often spit roasted with herbs.
Aragosta
Spiny lobster from the Latina coast.
Bigné
Fried choux pastry balls filled with cream.
Carciofi alla giuda
Young tender artichokes fried and flattened.
Carciofi alla romana
Stuffed artichokes stewed in oil.
Coda alla vaccinara
Oxtail in tomato sauce with celery.

Sicilian style fish steaks (page 77)

Red mullet Venetian style (page 35)

Crostini alla provatura

Bread slices topped with provatura cheese baked with an anchovy and oil sauce poured over them.

Fettuccine

Ribbon pasta, served in many ways.

Filetti di baccalà

Dried cod, battered and fried.

Mazzancolle

Very large prawns, a speciality of Formia and Gaeta.

Maccheroni alla ciociara

Pasta with a sauce of fat bacon, ham and sliced sausage.

Maccheroni alla ricotta

Pasta with a well seasoned cream cheese sauce.

Suppli al ragù

Fried rice balls with meat sauce.

Testarelle di abbacchio

Roast lambs' heads flavoured with rosemary.

Trippa alla romana

Tripe in a mint flavoured tomato sauce with Pecorino cheese.

CHEESES

Pecorino romano

Hard sheeps' milk cheese, very tasty and, grated, a good substitute for Parmesan.

Provolone

Mild when young but sharp and spicy when older. Originally made from buffaloes' milk, now usually from cows' milk.

Ricotta

Soft, unsalted ewes' milk cheese (page 6).

Scamorza

Similar to Mozzarella but made with cows' milk.

FONDI DI CARCIOFI IN SALSA
Antipasto of artichoke hearts

A simple meal starter using canned or bottled artichoke hearts.

Serves 3–4

IMPERIAL/METRIC	AMERICAN
3–4 tablespoons olive oil	4–5 tablespoons olive oil
1 tablespoon lemon juice	1 tablespoon lemon juice
1 teaspoon grated onion	1 teaspoon grated onion
salt and pepper	salt and pepper
1 teaspoon chopped parsley	1 teaspoon chopped parsley
½ teaspoon chopped marjoram	½ teaspoon chopped marjoram
12 small cooked artichoke hearts	12 small cooked artichoke hearts

In a bowl mix together the oil, lemon juice, onion and seasonings to taste. Finely chop the fresh parsley and marjoram and add to the bowl with the well drained artichoke hearts. Toss lightly and chill for an hour, turning occasionally. Serve in individual dishes.

STRACCIATELLA
'Ragged' egg soup

A light and nourishing soup whose name derives from the soft flakes formed by the egg. Italians make it with the broth left after boiling a fowl.

Serves 4–6

IMPERIAL/METRIC	AMERICAN
2 pints/generous 1 litre chicken broth	5 cups chicken broth
2 eggs	2 eggs
2 tablespoons fine semolina	3 tablespoons fine semolina flour
2 oz./50 g. grated Parmesan	½ cup grated Parmesan
chopped parsley	chopped parsley
grated nutmeg	grated nutmeg
salt and pepper	salt and pepper

Heat all but 3 tablespoons of the broth to boiling point. In a basin, beat together the eggs, semolina, cheese, parsley, shake of nutmeg and the 3 tablespoons of broth. Stirring continuously with a fork, add this to the pan of broth, season to taste and bring *just* to boiling point. *Immediately* pour into a warm tureen or soup bowls. Hand more grated Parmesan separately.

GNOCCHI DI SEMOLINO
Semolina gnocchi

In Rome semolina gnocchi are preferred to the potato gnocchi popular elsewhere. It's a very adaptable recipe – tasty Cheddar cheese is a good substitute for Parmesan, you can add a little finely chopped ham or even serve them with a tomato sauce.

Serves 4

IMPERIAL/METRIC	AMERICAN
1 pint/6 dl. milk	2½ cups milk
salt and pepper	salt and pepper
grated nutmeg	grated nutmeg
4 oz./100 g. fine semolina	⅔ cup fine semolina flour
3 oz./75 g. grated Parmesan	¾ cup grated Parmesan
2 small eggs	2 eggs
1½ oz./40 g. butter	3 tablespoons butter

Heat the milk with seasoning and nutmeg to taste. Shower in the semolina, stirring all the time. Stir until boiling, then cook *gently* for 2–3 minutes or until the spoon will stand up unsupported in the centre of the mixture. Off the heat, stir in 2 oz. (50 g.) of the cheese and the beaten eggs. Return to the heat and cook, stirring, for 1 minute. Check seasoning. In a flat oiled tin, spread the mixture about ⅓ inch (1½ cm.) thick. Cover and leave until cold and firm. Cut into rounds or squares about 1½ inches (4 cm.) across and arrange slightly overlapping in circles or rows in a buttered, shallow flameproof dish of 7–8 inches (18–20 cm.) diameter (or in 4 individual dishes). Dot evenly with butter and sprinkle with the remaining cheese. Before serving, heat through under a moderate grill then increase the heat until the surface is golden. Serve at once.

SPAGHETTI ALLA MATRICIANA
Spaghetti with bacon, pepper and tomatoes

This version of a favourite Roman recipe was given to me by a famous Italian chef. Look for it in the small family restaurants of the Trastevere district.

Serves 4

IMPERIAL/METRIC	AMERICAN
1 small red pepper	1 small red sweet pepper
12 oz./350 g. ripe tomatoes	¾ lb. ripe tomatoes
6 oz./175 g. unsmoked fat bacon	6 oz. unsmoked fat bacon slices
3 oz./75 g. onion, chopped	¾ cup chopped onion
12 oz./350 g. spaghetti	¾ lb. spaghetti
salt and black pepper	salt and black pepper
2 oz./50 g. grated Pecorino or Parmesan	½ cup grated Pecorino or Parmesan

Illustrated in colour on page 56

Halve the pepper, deseed and chop finely. Peel the tomatoes, squeeze out the seeds and chop the flesh. Cut the bacon into thin strips and fry slowly in a thick saucepan until *crisp*; remove from the pan and keep hot. In 1 tablespoon of the bacon fat, gently fry the onion and pepper until beginning to soften then add the tomatoes and cook rapidly for 5 to 6 minutes only. This can all be done in advance. Cook the spaghetti in plenty of boiling, salted water until 'al dente'. Sprinkle the cheese over the bottom of a serving dish, add the well drained spaghetti and toss until the cheese has melted. Meanwhile reheat the sauce, add the bacon, season liberally with pepper and pile in the centre of the spaghetti. Serve immediately, *without* additional cheese.

Lamb with sweet peppers (page 67)

SUPPLÌ AL TELEFONO
'Telephone wire' rice balls

Supplì are rice balls containing Mozzarella cheese which pulls into long 'wires' when the supplì are pulled apart – hence the name. Other good 'melting' cheeses such as Bel Paese can be used but the 'wires' will be missing.

Serves 3

IMPERIAL/METRIC	AMERICAN
half recipe risotto (page 11)*	half recipe risotto (page 11) *
1 large egg	1 egg
2 oz./50 g. Mozzarella cheese, diced	⅓ cup diced Mozzarella cheese
2 oz./50 g. lean ham	2 oz. lean cured ham
dry breadcrumbs	dried bread crumbs
oil for frying	oil for frying

*Can be left-over or freshly made and cooled.

The risotto should be moist but not wet. Beat the egg lightly and stir into the risotto to bind it. Cut the cheese and ham into ¼ inch (½ cm.) dice. Flatten a tablespoonful of rice in the palm of one hand, put 3 pieces of cheese and ham in the centre and cover with another spoonful of rice. Form into a ball completely enclosing the filling. Coat the balls thickly with breadcrumbs then leave to firm up in the refrigerator. Fry 4 or 5 at a time in hot deep oil, 375°F., 190°C., until golden outside and cheese melted inside – about 5 minutes. Drain on absorbent paper and keep hot in the oven until all have been cooked.

SFORMATO DI PISELLI E PROSCIUTTO
Pea and ham mould

Although more substantial than a soufflé, a sformato makes a deliciously light and unusual supper dish. You can omit the ham and serve the mould surrounded with small pieces of meat or fish, sausages or poached eggs.

Serves 4

IMPERIAL/METRIC	AMERICAN
about 2 oz./50 g. butter	about ¼ cup butter
2 oz./50 g. onion, sliced	½ cup sliced onion
1 lb./450 g. frozen peas	3 cups frozen peas
salt and pepper	salt and pepper
1 oz./25 g. flour	¼ cup all-purpose flour
7 fl. oz./2 dl. hot milk	generous ¾ cup hot milk
2 oz./50 g. cooked ham	2 oz. cooked cured ham
1 oz./25 g. grated Parmesan	¼ cup grated Parmesan
3 eggs, separated	3 eggs, separated
½ pint/3 dl. tomato sauce (page 9)	1¼ cups tomato sauce (page 9)

Illustrated in colour on page 28

Well butter a charlotte mould or soufflé dish of at least 2 pint (generous 1 litre, 5 cup) capacity. Melt ½ oz. (15 g.) butter in a saucepan, fry the onion gently until soft, then add the peas, seasoning and water to cover. Bring to the boil, cover and simmer until tender; then strain and purée in an electric blender or rub through a sieve. Meanwhile, melt 1 oz. (25 g.) butter in a large saucepan, stir in the flour and cook for a minute, then add the milk and stir briskly and heat until a very thick sauce forms. Off the heat, stir in the finely chopped ham, cheese, egg yolks and, finally, the pea purée; mix thoroughly. Lastly whisk the egg whites until stiff then fold lightly into the mixture. Turn into the prepared mould. Cover with foil and place in a baking tin with hot water to reach halfway up the mould. Cook in an oven, preheated to 350°F., 180°C., Gas Mark 4, until firm in the centre – about 1 hour. Rest for a few minutes, then unmould and serve with the tomato sauce poured over.

SPAGHETTI ALLA CARBONARA
Spaghetti with bacon and egg

Serves 4

IMPERIAL/METRIC	AMERICAN
12 oz./350 g. spaghetti	¾ lb. spaghetti
6 oz./175 g. unsmoked streaky bacon rashers	6 oz. unsmoked bacon slices
3 eggs	3 eggs
2 tablespoons cream	3 tablespoons cream
1 oz./25 g. grated Parmesan	¼ cup grated Parmesan
ground black pepper	ground black pepper
1 oz./25 g. butter	2 tablespoons butter

Cook the spaghetti in plenty of fast boiling, salted water until tender but 'al dente', about 10 minutes, then drain thoroughly. Meanwhile cut the bacon into ½-inch (1-cm.) pieces and fry gently until crisp. Beat the eggs in a bowl with the cream, cheese and a liberal seasoning of pepper. Heat the butter in a large saucepan, add the egg mix and stir until it *begins* to thicken. Immediately, add the fried bacon and the spaghetti and mix quickly and lightly.

SPEZZATINO DI POLLO CON PEPERONI
Chicken with peppers

Serves 4

IMPERIAL/METRIC	AMERICAN
4 chicken quarters	4 chicken quarters
flour, salt	flour, salt
4 tablespoons olive oil	⅓ cup olive oil
3 oz./75 g. onion, chopped	¾ cup chopped onion
1 clove garlic, crushed	1 clove garlic, crushed
1 lb./½ kg. ripe tomatoes	1 lb. ripe tomatoes
1 large green pepper	1 large green sweet pepper
1 oz./25 g. grated Parmesan	¼ cup grated Parmesan
1 tablespoon chopped fresh basil or parsley	1 tablespoon chopped fresh basil or parsley

Dust the chicken pieces with flour and sprinkle with salt. Heat 3 tablespoons oil in a wide saucepan and stir in the onion and garlic. Add the chicken and fry over gentle heat until golden, about 15 minutes, stirring and turning as necessary. Skin and quarter the tomatoes, add to the pan, cover and *simmer* for 20 minutes. Meanwhile halve and deseed the pepper and cut into ½-inch (1-cm.) strips. Fry gently for 10 minutes in the remaining olive oil, then add to the chicken and continue cooking gently for another 5–10 minutes. Dish the chicken. If necessary reduce the sauce by rapid boiling, then stir in the cheese and herbs. Check the seasoning and pour over the chicken.

SALTIMBOCCA
Veal with ham and sage

Fresh sage leaves give this simple dish its character. Use *thin* slices of raw gammon if prosciutto is not available.

Serves 4

IMPERIAL/METRIC	AMERICAN
8 thin slices veal fillet, about 2 oz./50 g. each	8 thin slices veal round, about 2 oz. each
ground black pepper	ground black pepper
8 sage leaves	8 sage leaves
8 small slices raw prosciutto	8 small slices raw prosciutto or cured ham
about 2 oz./50 g. butter	about ¼ cup butter
6 tablespoons white wine or Marsala	½ cup white wine or Marsala

Beat the slices of veal out until very thin and about 3 inches (7½ cm.) across. Season with pepper and lay a sage leaf on each piece. Cut the ham in similar size pieces, lay on top and secure the 'sandwich' with a cocktail stick. Dust with flour. Melt 1 oz. (25 g., 2 tablespoons) butter in a large frying pan and gently fry the *saltimbocca*, as many as will lay flat in the pan, until golden and cooked through – about 10 minutes in all. Arrange on a serving dish, remove the cocktail sticks and keep hot until all are cooked. (It is quicker if you use two pans.) Add the wine or Marsala to the pan, plus any remaining butter, and boil rapidly, stirring to dissolve the pan juices. When well reduced, pour over the *saltimbocca* and serve at once.

AGNELLO CON PEPERONI
Lamb with sweet peppers

Serves 4

IMPERIAL/METRIC	AMERICAN
2 lb./1 kg. lamb*	2 lb. lamb*
salt and pepper	salt and pepper
little flour	little flour
2 cloves garlic	2 cloves garlic
2 tablespoons olive oil	3 tablespoons olive oil
½ pint/3 dl. white wine	1¼ cups white wine
6 sweet peppers**	6 sweet peppers**
8 oz./¼ kg. ripe tomatoes	½ lb. ripe tomatoes
1 bay leaf	1 bay leaf

*Best end and middle neck (U.S. rib roast).
**Red, green and yellow if possible.

Cut the meat into neat pieces, sprinkle with salt and pepper and dust with flour. Peel and crush the garlic. Heat the oil and garlic in a wide flameproof casserole, add the meat and fry until lightly browned, stirring frequently. Add the wine and bubble briskly until reduced by a third. Cut the peppers into quarters, discard seeds and pith and rinse in cold water. Peel and quarter the tomatoes. Add both to the lamb with the bay leaf. Cover and simmer over *low* heat for about 45 minutes. Check the seasoning and serve from the casserole, with creamed potatoes.
Illustrated in colour on page 64

ABBACCHIO BRODETTATO
Baby lamb with egg and lemon sauce

Lean shoulder of lamb trimmed of fat is a good cut for this pleasant dish. A little fresh marjoram chopped with the parsley is a very Roman touch.

Serves 4

IMPERIAL/METRIC	AMERICAN
1¼ lb./600 g. boneless lamb	1¼ lb. boneless lamb
2 oz./50 g. unsmoked bacon	2 oz. unsmoked bacon
1 oz./25 g. lard	2 tablespoons lard
2 oz./50 g. onion, chopped	½ cup chopped onion
salt and pepper	salt and pepper
1 oz./25 g. flour	¼ cup all-purpose flour
4 tablespoons white wine	⅓ cup white wine
½ pint/3 dl. stock or water	1¼ cups stock or water
2 egg yolks	2 egg yolks
1 tablespoon lemon juice	1 tablespoon lemon juice
little chopped parsley	little chopped parsley

Cut the lamb into 1-inch (2½-cm.) cubes and the bacon into dice. Melt the lard in a saucepan and fry the lamb, bacon and onion together until beginning to colour. Sprinkle in the seasoning and flour and cook, stirring, for a minute or so. Add the wine and boil briskly until almost evaporated then stir in the stock or water and bring to the boil. Cover the pan tightly and *simmer gently* for 45 minutes, stirring occasionally. Skim off any surface fat and should the liquid have evaporated make up to the original amount. Shortly before serving, beat together the egg yolks, lemon juice and parsley and stir in 2 tablespoons of hot lamb stock. Stir into the *brodettato* and cook over *low* heat, stirring constantly, until the egg has thickened the sauce. *Do not allow to boil.* Serve at once.

CANNELLONI RIPIENI DI AGNELLO
Cannelloni stuffed with lamb

Serves 3–4

IMPERIAL/METRIC	AMERICAN
2 oz./50 g. mushrooms	½ cup mushrooms
8–9 oblong green or white lasagne	8–9 oblong green or white lasagne
2 oz./50 g. butter	¼ cup butter
8 oz./225 g. cooked minced lamb	1 cup cooked ground lamb
2 level tablespoons grated Parmesan	3 level tablespoons grated Parmesan
salt and pepper	salt and pepper
grated nutmeg	grated nutmeg
little stock	little stock
½ pint/3 dl. Béchamel sauce (page 9)	1¼ cups Béchamel sauce (page 9)
1 tablespoon grated cheese	1 tablespoon grated cheese

For the topping

IMPERIAL/METRIC	AMERICAN
1 oz./25 g. butter	2 tablespoons butter
grated Parmesan	grated Parmesan

Illustrated on the jacket

Wash and finely chop the mushrooms. Cook the lasagne in boiling salted water for 5 minutes (or according to directions on the packet) then drain and lay the lasagne flat ready for stuffing. Meanwhile, melt the butter and fry the mushrooms gently for 2–3 minutes. Stir in the lamb, cheese, seasoning, nutmeg to taste and enough stock to make a fairly soft mixture. Lay some of the filling across each piece of pasta then roll up to form cannelloni. If using bought round cannelloni, with the aid of a teaspoon fill each cannelloni with the stuffing. This has to be done carefully as the cannelloni is inclined to split if handled too roughly. Arrange in a single layer in a greased ovenproof dish. Make the Béchamel sauce using stock instead of milk and thinning to a pouring consistency; add the cheese. Pour the sauce over the cannelloni, dot with butter and sprinkle thickly with Parmesan cheese. Put into a hot oven (425°F., 220°C., Gas Mark 7) until lightly browned.

CIPPOLLINE IN AGRODOLCE
Onions in sweet-sour sauce

Serves 4

IMPERIAL/METRIC	AMERICAN
1 lb./½ kg. button onions	1 lb. tiny onions
2 tablespoons oil	3 tablespoons oil
1 bay leaf	1 bay leaf
2 cloves	2 cloves
2 tablespoons wine vinegar	3 tablespoons wine vinegar
1 tablespoon sugar	1 tablespoon sugar

Cook the unpeeled onions in boiling, salted water for 10 minutes. Drain and when cool enough to handle, remove the skins. Heat the oil with the bay leaf and cloves, add the onions and cook gently for 5 minutes, stirring frequently. Add the vinegar and sugar and continue cooking gently until the sauce is syrupy and the onions tender. Serve hot as a vegetable or cold as part of a first course.

SPINACI ALLA ROMANA
Roman style spinach

Serves 3–4

IMPERIAL/METRIC	AMERICAN
1 oz./25 g. sultanas	3 tablespoons seedless white raisins
1½ lb./¾ kg. spinach	1½ lb. spinach
1 oz./25 g. cooked ham	1 oz. cooked cured ham
1 oz./25 g. butter	2 tablespoons butter
1 tablespoon pine nuts	1 tablespoon pine nuts
salt and pepper	salt and pepper

To garnish

IMPERIAL/METRIC	AMERICAN
triangles fried bread	triangles fried bread

Cover the sultanas with warm water and leave to swell. Wash the spinach thoroughly. Put into a large pan without additional water and cook, covered, until tender – about 10 minutes. Drain and press to extract as much water as possible. Meanwhile cut the ham into fine strips and heat gently in a saucepan with the melted butter. Add spinach, drained sultanas, nuts and seasoning to taste. Stir well, cover and leave over low heat for 5 minutes. Serve in a dish surrounded with triangles of crisply fried bread.

ПAPLES AПD THE SOUTH

The cooking of the South is colourful, zestful and unsophisticated. It springs directly from the local raw materials so expect to find mainly dishes containing pasta, tomatoes, olives and olive oil, garlic, herbs, vegetables, cheese and fish of all kinds. You are now in the heart of pasta land, and spaghetti and macaroni are practically synonymous with Naples – the home of manufactured pasta. But as you travel around Campania, Apulia, Calabria and Basilicata you'll meet many pasta shapes that are unknown in other regions. In Apulia, for instance, *recchietelle* (little ears) are greatly valued because the sauce gets caught up inside them making a much tastier dish! This is the home of Mozzarella cheese, still made here from buffaloes' milk instead of cows' milk as in the rest of Italy. Aubergine, sweet peppers and zucchini (courgette) abound, and there is an abundance of fresh fruit of all kinds. As well as the classic Neapolitan pizza of bread dough topped with tomatoes, Mozzarella cheese, anchovies and olives, there are local pizza specialities containing salami, mushrooms or shellfish. For the sweet tooth, there are numerous small cakes, biscuits and pastries and every festival has its own specialities.

THE WINES

A great deal of wine is produced throughout this huge area, especially in Apulia and Campania. The wines are rather variable and many of the same name come in red, white or rosato varieties. Most of the reds need some bottle age.

White wines

Castel del monte
A fresh white wine that has earned a DOC label.
Ciro
Full, flowery but dry wine from Calabria.
Ishia
Dry, balanced wine, good with fish.
Lachrima Christi
Famous name wine that can be either dry or sweet. (Also a red and rosato variety.)
Locorotondo
Pale wine which improves with age.
San severo
Dry, fresh wine.

Red wines

Aglianico
Deep coloured dry wine, needs bottle age.
Castel del monte
Dry wine which improves with age.
Ciro
Big robust wine, needs bottle age.
Ishia red
Dry and mellow when suitably aged.

SOME FOOD SPECIALITIES

Calzoni
Kind of folded pizza, fried or baked.
Capitone
Large eel, roasted or marinated and fried.
Capretto ripieno
Kid stuffed with herbs and spices.
Fritto misto
Mixture of fish, cheese, cauliflower, potatoes and sweetbreads, deep fried.

Panzerotti	*Sopressata*
Kind of stuffed pasta.	Garlic flavoured sausage.
Polpi alla luciana	*Turcinielli*
Octopus in olive oil, parsley and ginger sauce.	Pasta in the shape of little spirals.
Recchietelle	*Zuppa alla marinara*
Pasta in shape of little ears.	Fish stew.
Sartù	*Zuppa di vongole*
Savoury rice dish with many additions.	Clam stew.
Sfogliatliatella	
Flaky pastry filled with cream cheese and candied fruits.	

COZZE GRATINATE
Mussels au gratin

Serves 4

IMPERIAL/METRIC	AMERICAN
4 pints/2¼ litres mussels	5 pints mussels
2 cloves garlic, peeled	2 cloves garlic, peeled
bunch parsley	bunch parsley
1 oz./25 g. fine soft breadcrumbs	½ cup fine soft bread crumbs
4 tablespoons olive oil	⅓ cup olive oil
½ teaspoon wine vinegar	½ teaspoon wine vinegar

Scrape and clean the mussels carefully in cold water, discarding any that do not close tightly when tapped. Wash again in several changes of cold water. Meanwhile, chop finely the garlic and parsley and mix evenly with the breadcrumbs. Preheat a hot oven (450°F., 230°C., Gas Mark 8). Put the drained mussels into a heavy saucepan, cover and heat sharply, shaking the pan frequently until the mussels open in about 5–6 minutes. Remove from the heat and discard the top shell from each mussel. Arrange the mussels, shell downwards and side by side, in one large shallow gratin dish or 4 small ones. Cover each mussel with a little of the breadcrumb mixture and moisten with the oil mixed with the vinegar. Cook near the top of the oven for 5 minutes until just tinged with brown. Don't overcook or the mussels will toughen.

Illustrated in colour on page 32

TRENETTE CON AGLIO E OLIO
Ribbon pasta with oil and garlic

This simple dish is often made with spaghetti, but the Neapolitan who gave me the recipe prefers to use a fine ribbon pasta such as *trenette* or *linguine*.

Serves 4

IMPERIAL/METRIC	AMERICAN
12 oz./350 g. trenette	¾ lb. trenette
salt	salt
2 cloves garlic	2 cloves garlic
5 tablespoons olive oil	6 tablespoons olive oil
ground black pepper	ground black pepper
2 tablespoons chopped parsley	3 tablespoons chopped parsley

Cook the pasta in plenty of well salted, boiling water until just 'al dente'. Drain thoroughly and put into a hot serving dish. Meanwhile peel and crush two fat cloves of garlic and put into a small saucepan with a fine quality olive oil and several grinds of pepper. Warm the oil and garlic but do not fry it. When the oil is well flavoured, strain it over the pasta and add the parsley. Toss together thoroughly and serve at once – without cheese in the true Neapolitan manner. My friend added that he liked to strain the oil to remove the garlic, but his wife liked the garlic left in!

MACCHERONI AL FORNO
Savoury baked macaroni

Maccheroni is a generic word covering all types of pasta. For this substantial family dish, any hollow tubular shape in short 1-inch (2½-cm.) lengths can be used.

Serves 4

IMPERIAL/METRIC	AMERICAN
4 rashers streaky bacon	4 bacon slices
1 tablespoon olive oil	1 tablespoon olive oil
3 oz./75 g. onion, chopped	¾ cup chopped onion
1 (14 oz./400 g.) can tomatoes	1 (14 oz.) can tomatoes
salt and pepper	salt and pepper
10 oz./275 g. short macaroni	2½ cups short macaroni
grated Parmesan	grated Parmesan

Derind and chop the bacon. Heat the oil in a saucepan and fry the bacon and onion gently for 5 minutes. Add the tomatoes and their liquid with seasoning to taste and simmer, covered, for 20 to 30 minutes until a thin sauce is formed. Stir it from time to time. Meanwhile cook the macaroni in plenty of boiling, salted water until *almost* tender, about 10 minutes, then drain and turn into an oiled pie dish. Pour the tomato sauce over the macaroni and sprinkle the surface thickly with cheese. Bake in a moderate oven (350°F., 180°C., Gas Mark 4) for 15–20 minutes until the cheese is melted and golden.

TONNO FRESCO AL POMODORI
Fresh tunny with tomatoes

Serves 4

IMPERIAL/METRIC	AMERICAN
1 small onion	1 small onion
2 cloves garlic	2 cloves garlic
olive oil	olive oil
3 fillets anchovy	3 fillets anchovy
5 tablespoons white wine	6 tablespoons white wine
1½ lb./¾ kg. ripe tomatoes	1½ lb. ripe tomatoes
1 bay leaf	1 bayleaf
pepper and salt	pepper and salt
1¼ lb./600 g. piece fresh tunny fish*	1¼ lb. piece fresh tuna fish
2 oz./50 g. black olives	scant ½ cup ripe olives

* Swordfish, or any firm fish could be used instead.

Peel and chop the onion and garlic. Heat 2 tablespoons oil in a saucepan, fry the onion and garlic gently until soft then add the mashed anchovy fillets and the wine. Bubble briskly until the wine has almost evaporated. Skin and roughly chop the tomatoes and add to the pan with the bay leaf and pepper to taste. Simmer until reduced to a sauce consistency. Meanwhile season the piece of tunny fish and dust with flour. Heat 1½ tablespoons of oil in a flameproof casserole and fry the tunny slowly until golden both sides. Pour the tomato sauce over it, cover and simmer gently for 20–30 minutes. Add the olives 5 minutes before serving.

SALSA PIZZAIOLA
Fresh tomato sauce

A colourful sauce to cheer up second grade steak, chops or slices of pork or lamb; adjusting the cooking time to the thickness and quality of the meat. Good with portions of white fish, too.

Serves 3–4

IMPERIAL/METRIC	AMERICAN
3 cloves garlic	3 cloves garlic
1¼ lb./600 g. ripe tomatoes	1¼ lb. ripe tomatoes
2 tablespoons olive oil	3 tablespoons olive oil
salt and black pepper	salt and black pepper
fresh basil or dried oregano	fresh basil or dried oregano

Peel and slice the garlic. Skin, deseed and roughly chop the tomatoes. Heat the oil and garlic slowly in a saucepan, add the tomatoes with salt and pepper to taste. Cook briskly for about 5 minutes, until the ingredients have softened but not become a pulp. Add roughly torn basil or dried oregano to taste.

BISTECCA ALLA PIZZAIOLA
Beef steak with tomato sauce

Allow 1 thinnish steak, rump or rib, for each person and season with pepper and salt. Cover the base of a wide pan with a thin film of olive oil and when hot fry the steaks quickly until lightly browned on each side and half cooked. Top each steak with a thick layer of *pizzaiola* sauce, cover the pan and cook over *low* heat for another 10 minutes. Snip a little fresh parsley over before serving.

ROGNONI TRIFOLATI
Sautéed kidneys

Serves 4

IMPERIAL/METRIC	AMERICAN
1 lb./½ kg. veal kidneys	1 lb. veal kidneys
2 teaspoons flour	2 teaspoons flour
salt and pepper	salt and pepper
1 oz./25 g. butter	2 tablespoons butter
1 tablespoon oil	1 tablespoon oil
1 clove garlic	1 clove garlic
little chopped parsley	little chopped parsley
1 tablespoon lemon juice	1 tablespoon lemon juice
To garnish	
fried bread	fried bread

Remove all fat from the kidneys and peel off the thin skin. Cut them into thin slices and toss these with the flour and a little seasoning. Gently heat the butter and oil in a large frying pan with the peeled clove of garlic for 2 minutes; discard the garlic. Add the kidneys to the pan and cook over moderate heat, turning the slices frequently for 3–5 minutes. Add the parsley and lemon juice, stir around quickly and turn into a hot serving dish. Garnish with small triangles of bread, fried crisp and golden in oil and butter.

PEPERONI RIPIENI
Stuffed sweet peppers

This is a typical meatless family recipe, but rice stuffings containing small amounts of minced meat are popular too. It depends on what's in the larder, the Neapolitans say.

Serves 4

IMPERIAL/METRIC	AMERICAN
4 large sweet peppers*	4 large sweet peppers*
1 tablespoon sultanas	1 tablespoon seedless white raisins
4 oz./100 g. white bread	4 oz. white bread
little milk	little milk
8 anchovy fillets	8 anchovy fillets
1 tablespoon chopped parsley	1 tablespoon chopped parsley
1 tablespoon capers	1 tablespoon capers
2 cloves garlic, peeled	2 cloves garlic, peeled
black olives (optional)	ripe olives (optional)
olive oil	olive oil

*Red, yellow, green, or mixed colours.

Cut the tops off the peppers and discard all seeds and pith; rinse in cold water. Cover the sultanas with warm water and leave to plump. Soak the bread in milk until soft and then squeeze dry. Put the bread into a basin and add the chopped anchovy fillets, parsley, capers, drained sultanas, crushed garlic, stoned and chopped olives if used, and 2 tablespoons of olive oil; mix thoroughly and season if necessary. Fill into the peppers and stand upright in a deep casserole. Pour a little oil over each, cover the casserole and cook in a moderate oven (325°F., 170°C., Gas Mark 3) for 45–50 minutes.

PARMIGIANA DI MELANZANE
Aubergine and cheese pie

Serves 4

IMPERIAL/METRIC	AMERICAN
4 aubergines	4 eggplants
salt	salt
1 recipe tomato sauce (page 9)	1 recipe tomato sauce (page 9)
little flour	little flour
olive oil	olive oil
ground black pepper	ground black pepper
6 oz./175 g. Mozzarella*	6 oz. Mozzarella*
2 oz./50 g. grated Parmesan	½ cup grated Parmesan
1 teaspoon dried basil	1 teaspoon dried basil
*Or use Bel Paese.	

Peel the aubergines and cut into ¼-inch (½-cm.) slices lengthwise. Sprinkle with salt and leave in a colander to drain for at least an hour. Make the tomato sauce. Rinse the aubergine slices, pat dry and dust with flour. Fry them in hot olive oil until golden on each side, then drain thoroughly on absorbent paper. Sprinkle with pepper. Slice the cheese thinly. In a deep ovenproof dish, arrange alternate layers of tomato sauce, fried aubergine, sliced cheese and Parmesan with a sprinkling of basil. Finish with a layer of sliced cheese and Parmesan. Bake in a moderately hot oven (400°F., 200°C., Gas Mark 6) for about 15 minutes, until hot through and bubbling.

INSALATA DI CARCIOFI
Salad of artichoke hearts

Serves 3

IMPERIAL/METRIC	AMERICAN
1 (14 oz./400 g.) can artichoke hearts	1 (14 oz.) can artichoke hearts
2 hard-boiled eggs	2 hard-cooked eggs
3 tomatoes, quartered	3 tomatoes, quartered
2 oz./50 g. black olives	⅓ cup ripe olives
For the dressing	
Capri salad dressing (page 74)	Capri salad dressing (page 74)
sprigs fresh parsley	sprigs fresh parsley

Quarter the artichoke hearts and cut the hard-boiled eggs into sixths. Arrange on a salad plate with the tomatoes and olives. Just before serving, sprinkle with the dressing and snip a little parsley over the top.

Illustrated in colour on page 49

INSALATA DI CAVOLFIORE
Cauliflower salad

Serves 4

IMPERIAL/METRIC	AMERICAN
1 large cauliflower	1 large cauliflower
salt and pepper	salt and pepper
6 anchovy fillets	6 anchovy fillets
1 tablespoon capers	1 tablespoon capers
1 tablespoon wine vinegar	1 tablespoon wine vinegar
3 tablespoons olive oil	scant ¼ cup olive oil
little chopped parsley	little chopped parsley
2 oz./50 g. black olives	⅓ cup ripe olives

Break the cauliflower into small flowerets and cook in boiling salted water until just tender, about 5 minutes. Drain, rinse under cold water and drain again. Chop the anchovy fillets. Rinse and drain the capers. Mix the vinegar, seasonings and oil in a salad bowl, carefully toss the cauliflower in it. Sprinkle with chopped anchovies, capers, parsley and stoned olives.

INSALATA ALLA CAPRICCOSA
Capri style salad

Serves 3–4

IMPERIAL/METRIC	AMERICAN
1 large lettuce	1 large head lettuce
1 yellow pepper	1 yellow sweet pepper
4 tomatoes, quartered	4 tomatoes, quartered
6 oz./175 g. cooked French beans	6 oz. cooked green beans
2 sticks celery, sliced	2 stalks celery, sliced
1 (7 oz./200 g.) can tuna fish	1 (7 oz.) can tuna fish
8 anchovy fillets	8 anchovy fillets
few black olives	few ripe olives
For the dressing	
1 tablespoon wine vinegar	1 tablespoon wine vinegar
salt and pepper	salt and pepper
1 clove garlic, crushed	1 clove garlic, crushed
4 tablespoons olive oil	⅓ cup olive oil

Wash, dry and crisp the lettuce. Halve, deseed and rinse the pepper then cut into fine strips. Line a salad bowl with lettuce and arrange the prepared vegetables casually on top. Add the tuna fish in large pieces criss-crossed with anchovy fillets. Scatter the olives over. Shake all the dressing ingredients together vigorously and sprinkle over the salad. Serve promptly.

INSALATA DI SEDANI E FINOCCHIO
Celery and fennel salad

Serves 3–4

IMPERIAL/METRIC	AMERICAN
1 small head celery	1 small bunch celery
8 oz./¼ kg. fennel bulbs	½ lb. fennel bulbs
2 eating apples	2 eating apples
2 teaspoons lemon juice	2 teaspoons lemon juice
mayonnaise (page 10)	mayonnaise (page 10)
1 hard-boiled egg	1 hard-cooked egg
parsley	parsley

Discard outer pieces of celery and fennel, and cut the rest into thin strips. Wash, dry and quarter the apples, discarding the cores. Cut into dice and toss with the lemon juice to prevent them browning. Mix the fennel, celery and apple together and arrange in a salad bowl. Mask with mayonnaise of coating consistency and garnish with slices of hard-boiled egg, pieces of celery or fennel leaf, and parsley.

CROSTINI ALLA NAPOLETANA
Neapolitan savouries

For these attractive and quickly made snacks, choose ¼ inch (½ cm.) thick slices from a day old sandwich loaf.

Serves 4

IMPERIAL/METRIC	AMERICAN
4 slices bread	4 slices bread
olive oil	olive oil
4 oz./100 g. Bel Paese cheese	¼ lb. Bel Paese cheese
8 anchovy fillets	8 anchovy fillets
2 firm tomatoes	2 firm tomatoes
ground black pepper	ground black pepper
dried oregano	dried oregano

Remove crusts and cut each slice in half cornerwise. Place the triangles on a well oiled baking sheet and cover each with a thin slice of cheese. Lay strips of anchovy over the cheese and top with a slice of tomato. Sprinkle with pepper and oregano and drizzle a teaspoonful of oil over each crostini. Bake in a preheated moderate oven (350°F., 180°C., Gas Mark 4) for 12–15 minutes, until the bread is crisp and the cheese melted.

SICILY

Farming is one of the chief means of sustenance on this sunny island, famous for its citrus fruits and wines. Olive trees, almond trees and prickly pears are familiar sights too, and a wide variety of vegetables are produced. The poor quality of the meat is more than made up for by excellent fish. The cooking generally is somewhat 'robust' and typical sauces for pasta are likely to include peppers, aubergine, garlic, capers, tomatoes, anchovies, olives and basil. Olive oil is used a great deal. But Sicilians have sweet tooths too, and sweet almonds and candied peel feature in many puddings, biscuits and pastries, often mixed with soft curd cheese. Sicily is credited with being the home of ices and of the famous Cassata, originally a feast day pudding of sponge cake layered with a rich cream studded with candied fruit and chocolate, covered with a plain or chocolate frosting. Nowadays an ice cream Cassata (gelato) has become the more familiar, certainly outside Italy.

THE WINES

Grapes and wine are known to have been honoured products of Sicily since about 2000 B.C. The island produces a great variety of wines, many of them with qualities which earn for them such descriptions as 'invigorating', 'exhilarating' and 'generous'. It is particularly famous as the home of Marsala.

White wines

Corvo di Salaparuta
Pleasant, balanced wine.
Etna (bianco)
Strong, fresh tasting wine.
Mamertino
Usually a semi-sweet wine, now rather scarce, but of ancient origin said to have been served to Caesar.

Red wines

Corvo di Salaparuta
Pleasant, light wine.
Etna (rosso)
Strong, rather volcanic flavour.
Faro
Dry all rounder which ages well.

Dessert wines

Malvasia di Lipari
Rich and luscious wine of ancient origin.
Moscato wines
Sweet golden wines from various parts of the island e.g. Moscato di Pantelleria.
Marsala
A dark, rich fortified wine which becomes drier with age. A popular dessert wine for some and for others a popular wine for cooking. The cheapest grade 'Marsala Fine' is for cooking, 'Marsala Vergine' which has been aged for at least five years is best for drinking.

SOME FOOD SPECIALITIES

Anelletti gratinati
Rings of cuttlefish, breadcrumbed and fried.
Bottarga
Tunny fish roe, cooked and served with oil and lemon.
Cannoli
Crisp pastry tubes with a Ricotta cream filling.
Caponata
Fried aubergine dish with tomatoes, onions and capers etc. Served cold.
Cuscucu
Fish soup.

Farsumagru
Breast of veal stuffed with minced meat, hard-boiled egg and spices.
Fichi d'india
Prickly pears.
Fruitta candita
Candied citrus fruit peel.
Frittura di sciabachedda
Assorted small fish, fried.
Maccu
Dried bean soup.
Pasta con le sarde
Pasta with a spicy tomato sauce containing sardines, nuts, fennel, sultanas, etc.
Pesce spada
Sword fish.

CHEESES

Caciocavallo
Small cheeses always tied in pairs. Pleasant table cheese when young, used for grating when mature.
Canestrato
Strong, salty ewes' milk cheese.
Ragusano
Delicate flavour when fresh, after 6 months a hard sharp cheese for grating.
Ricotta
White curd cheese much used in Sicilian pastries and puddings.

TAGLIERINA ALLA TAORIMINA
Pasta Taorimina style

Taglierina is a very narrow egg pasta. But any ribbon pasta would do for this typical Sicilian recipe which combines pasta and tomato sauce with vegetables. Use 1 lb. (½ kg.) fresh tomatoes instead of canned when in season.

Serves 4

IMPERIAL/METRIC	AMERICAN
2 aubergines	2 eggplants
olive oil	olive oil
1 onion, chopped	1 onion, chopped
2 cloves garlic, peeled	2 cloves garlic, peeled
1 (14 oz./400 g.) can tomatoes	1 (14 oz.) can tomatoes
salt and pepper	salt and pepper
sugar	sugar
fresh basil	fresh basil
12 oz./350 g. ribbon pasta	¾ lb. ribbon pasta
grated Parmesan	grated Parmesan

Cut the aubergines into ¼-inch (½-cm.) slices, sprinkle with salt and leave in a colander to drain for 1 hour. Heat 1½ tablespoons oil in a saucepan and fry the onion and sliced garlic *gently* until soft. Add the tomatoes and their juice plus seasonings of salt, pepper and sugar. Cover and simmer for 30–40 minutes until reduced to a sauce consistency. Add a few roughly torn up basil leaves if available. Drain and dry the aubergine slices and fry a few at a time in hot olive oil until tender and golden; drain and keep warm. Cook the pasta in plenty of fast boiling, salted water until tender but 'al dente'; drain and toss with a spoonful of olive oil until glistening. Pile on a serving dish, pour the sauce over and arrange the aubergine around. Sprinkle with Parmesan and hand more separately.

INSALATA DI POMODORI
Tomato salad

Italians choose firm, slightly green and under-ripe tomatoes to ensure a crisp and fresh tasting salad.

Serves 4

IMPERIAL/METRIC	AMERICAN
6 large tomatoes	6 large tomatoes
salt and pepper	salt and pepper
1 clove garlic	1 clove garlic
2–3 tablespoons olive oil	3–4 tablespoons olive oil
chopped fresh herbs*	chopped fresh herbs*

* Basil when available, otherwise parsley and green onion tops.

Wash and dry the tomatoes and keep in the refrigerator until required. Cut into *thin* slices and arrange slightly overlapping on a flat serving dish. Season with salt and pepper. Peel and crush the garlic, mix with the oil and sprinkle evenly over the tomatoes. Scatter chopped herbs over the surface and serve right away.

PESCE ALLA SICILIANA
Sicilian style fish steaks

In Sicily sword fish or fresh tunny might be used, but it is a tasty way of cooking *any* firm white fish.

Serves 4

IMPERIAL/METRIC	AMERICAN
4 portions fresh fish	4 portions fresh fish
1 large onion	1 large onion
1 stick celery	1 stalk celery
2 tablespoons olive oil	3 tablespoons olive oil
4 ripe tomatoes	4 ripe tomatoes
6 tablespoons white wine	½ cup white wine
2 tablespoons water	3 tablespoons water
salt and pepper	salt and pepper
12 green olives	12 green olives
1 tablespoon capers	1 tablespoon capers

Illustrated in colour on page 60

Preheat a moderately hot oven (375°F., 190°C., Gas Mark 5). Arrange the fish portions side by side in an oiled, shallow ovenproof dish. Chop the onion and celery and fry gently in the oil in a saucepan for 5 minutes. Meanwhile peel, seed and chop the tomatoes, then add to the saucepan with wine, water and seasoning. Stir and simmer together for 5 minutes. Add the stoned and halved olives and the capers, pour evenly over the fish. Bake in the centre of the oven for about 25 minutes, basting occasionally. Serve hot in the same dish, sprinkled with parsley, if liked.

CONIGLIO CON OLIVE VERDI
Rabbit with green olives

Serves 4

IMPERIAL/METRIC	AMERICAN
1 medium rabbit	1 medium rabbit
4 oz./100 g. belly pork	¼ lb. fresh picnic shoulder of pork
1 tablespoon oil	1 tablespoon oil
2 onions, sliced	2 onions, sliced
1 tablespoon flour	1 tablespoon flour
¾ pint/½ litre stock or water	2 cups stock or water
1 bay leaf	1 bayleaf
½ teaspoon rosemary	½ teaspoon rosemary
salt and black pepper	salt and black pepper
2 oz./50 g. green olives	⅓ cup green olives
few capers (optional)	few capers (optional)

Wash, dry and joint the rabbit. Dice the pork and put into a flameproof casserole with the oil and onions. Fry gently together until the fat is running from the pork. Add the rabbit and fry until lightly browned all over, then sprinkle with flour and stir for another minute. Stir in the stock, add the bay leaf and rosemary with seasoning to taste. Cover tightly and simmer until tender – about 45 minutes. Add the olives, and capers if used, about 10 minutes before serving.

Illustrated in colour on page 52

SALSA DI CAPPERI ALL'OLIO
Caper and parsley dressing

A fresh and piquant dressing to serve with hot or cold poached fish, or cold chopped chicken or lamb.

Served 4

IMPERIAL/METRIC	AMERICAN
2 tablespoons capers	3 tablespoons capers
5 tablespoons olive oil	6 tablespoons olive oil
2 tablespoons lemon juice	3 tablespoons lemon juice
2 tablespoons chopped parsley	3 tablespoons chopped parsley

Drain and rinse the capers. Put all the ingredients into a screw top jar and shake together until well blended. Shake again immediately before using.

ZABAIONE
Zabaione

Serves 4

IMPERIAL/METRIC	AMERICAN
4 egg yolks*	4 egg yolks*
2 oz./50 g. castor sugar	$\frac{1}{4}$ cup sugar
8 tablespoons Marsala	$\frac{2}{3}$ cup Marsala
To serve	
sponge finger biscuits	ladyfingers

* One egg white may be added.

Put the egg yolks and sugar into a basin and whisk until pale and frothy. Whisk in the Marsala. Rest the basin over a pan of almost boiling water, making sure the water does not touch the basin. Whisk continually until the mixture rises in the basin and becomes a thick foam throughout. This will take from 7 to 10 minutes for this quantity. Pour into wine glasses and serve at once.

GELATO DI TUTTI FRUTTI
Candied fruit ice cream

Serves 4–6

IMPERIAL/METRIC	AMERICAN
3 egg yolks	3 egg yolks
3 oz./75 g. castor sugar	6 tablespoons sugar
2–3 drops vanilla essence	2–3 drops vanilla extract
$\frac{1}{2}$ pint/3 dl. milk	$1\frac{1}{4}$ cups milk
1 oz./25 g. candied peel	3 tablespoons candied peel
1 oz./25 g. glacé pineapple	3 tablespoons candied pineapple
6 red glacé cherries	6 red candied cherries
1 inch (2$\frac{1}{2}$ cm.) angelica	1 inch candied angelica
$\frac{1}{4}$ pint/1$\frac{1}{2}$ dl. double cream	$\frac{2}{3}$ cup whipping cream
To decorate	
whipped cream	whipped cream
glacé fruits	candied fruits

Note If the candied fruit shows signs of sinking to the bottom, turn the ice into a basin when partially frozen and whisk thoroughly before returning to the freezer.

Turn the refrigerator to the coldest setting. Put the egg yolks, sugar and vanilla into a basin and mix thoroughly with a wooden spoon. Heat the milk *almost* to boiling point, then pour slowly on to the egg mixture stirring all the time. Strain back into the rinsed saucepan, cook over *low* heat stirring continuously until the mixture thickens enough to coat the back of the spoon. Don't allow to boil or the custard may curdle. (If you have one it is safer but slower to do this in a double saucepan.) Turn immediately into a shallow container and leave until cold. Cover and freeze until firm but not hard. Meanwhile chop all the candied fruits. When the ice cream is firm, turn it into a chilled basin. In another basin whisk the cream until thick then fold in the chopped fruits. Stir this mixture lightly into the ice cream. Turn mixture into a small loaf tin, basin or jelly mould of 1$\frac{1}{4}$ pint ($\frac{3}{4}$ litre, 3 cups) capacity. Cover and continue freezing until hard. Return the refrigerator to its normal setting, leaving the ice cream in the freezing compartment to mature until serving time. To serve, unmould the ice and decorate.

GRANITA DI LIMONE
Lemon water ice

Italian water ices melt quickly so serve them in tall glasses with a spoon and a straw.

Serves 3

IMPERIAL/METRIC	AMERICAN
4 large lemons	4 large lemons
4 oz./100 g. sugar	$\frac{1}{2}$ cup sugar
$\frac{3}{4}$ pint/4$\frac{1}{2}$ dl. water	2 cups water

Illustrated in colour on page 57

Wash one lemon and pare the rind thinly with a potato peeler. Heat the sugar and water gently until the sugar has *completely* dissolved, then add the rind and boil for 5 minutes exactly. Strain and leave until cold. Squeeze the juice from all 4 lemons, strain into the syrup and mix. Pour into an ice cube tray and freeze until firm.

INDEX